CYBER BLOCKADES

CYBER BLOCKADES

Alison Lawlor Russell

GEORGETOWN UNIVERSITY PRESS
Washington, DC

Library of Congress Cataloging-in-Publication Data

Russell, Alison Lawlor, author.
    Cyber blockades / Alison Lawlor Russell.
        pages   cm
    Includes bibliographical references and index.
        ISBN 978-1-62616-111-5 (hardcover : alk. paper) — ISBN 978-1-62616-112-2 (pbk. : alk. paper) — ISBN 978-1-62616-113-9 (ebook)
        1. Cyberterrorism.   2. Cyberterrorism—Prevention.   3. Cyberspace—Security measures.   4. Computer security.   I. Title.
    HV6773.15.C97R87   2014
    327.1'17—dc23
                                                                        2014011280

Cover design by Bruce Gore | Gore Studio, Inc. Image is by Shutterstock.

⊗ This book is printed on acid-free paper meeting the requirements of the American National Standard for Permanence in Paper for Printed Library Materials.

15 14   9 8 7 6 5 4 3 2   First printing

Printed in the United States of America

For my parents Joseph and Susan Lawlor,

&

for my husband Kevin

Contents

< vii >

Tables and Figure

Tables

Figure

< ix >

Acknowledgments

This research originally took form as a doctoral dissertation at the Fletcher School at Tufts University. I offer my profound thanks to Andrew Hess, Bill Martel, and Robert Pfaltzgraff Jr., who scrutinized the manuscript when it was in early forms and provided essential insights, critical analysis, and recommendations for improvement. Bernadette Kelly-Lecesse was a pillar of support. Many colleagues offered essential critiques and suggestions, particularly Chris Wrenn and Tom McCarthy, who encouraged me to write on this topic in the first place and generously shared their time and resources with me. This book could not have been written without the assistance of friends and colleagues who challenged my ideas and improved this work along the way, but any errors are my own.

< xi >

Abbreviations and Acronyms

CERT	Computer Emergency Response Team
DDoS	distributed denial of service
DoS	denial of service
EC	European Commission
EMP	electromagnetic pulse
ENP	European Neighbor Policy
EU	European Union
FSB	Federal Security Service (Russia)
GRU	General Staff of the Armed Forces (Russia)
HAMP	high-altitude electromagnetic pulse
HMP	high-power microwave
IP	internet protocol
IR	international relations
ISAF	International Security Assistance Force
ISP	internet service provider
IT	information technology
MAP	Membership Action Plan
Mbps	Megabits per second
NAC	North Atlantic Council
NATO	North Atlantic Treaty Organization

< xiii >

NFZ	no-fly zone
OSCE	Organization for Security and Cooperation in Europe
PCA	Partnership and Cooperation Agreement
RBN	Russian Business Network
SQL	search and query language
TCP SYN	transmission control protocol synchronize message
UAV	unmanned aerial vehicle
UK	United Kingdom
UN	United Nations
UNSCR	United Nations Security Council Resolution
US	United States
USSR	Union of Soviet Socialist Republics

CHAPTER 1

Networks of Power in the Information Society

Introduction

All of a sudden and without warning, cyberspace shut down. At first, people noticed that their desktops, laptops, and tablets were not responding to search requests or pinging with incoming email. Then they realized their smartphones had no data reception and no telephone service. Landlines (the plain, old telephone service) did not work either. The electrical grid and other basic services were compromised, affecting virtually everything, from digitally programmed home thermostats to gas stations to power plants to water treatment facilities. Financial markets cannot operate without a reliable connection to cyberspace, so the stock market closed early. Navigation and monitoring systems in cars, trains, and airplanes around the country simply did not work and there were massive closures of public transportation systems and airports. Most businesses closed down because they could not access their databases or execute transactions in a reliable fashion.

The government was alarmed because it was operating in the dark; its systems were down in offices around the country and it could not receive any information from beyond its borders. In the previous weeks and days the government had entered a period of heightened tensions with an adversary and received threats of attack by foreign forces. But now the government could not send or receive information from beyond its borders, even from its own embassies and troops stationed abroad. It could not access the government-controlled, secure, closed networks or satellite systems to get a visual look at what, if anything, was happening in and around the country.

< 1 >

Computer experts were working furiously to determine the origin of what they realized was the largest cyber attack in history, but they were working with limited capabilities within the borders of the target state and could not receive information or help from outside of the country. No one knew how long the situation would last or what they should do in the meantime. Banks and automatic teller machines could not function and credit cards would not work, so people were limited to the cash they had in their pockets when they left the house that morning, the food in the pantry, and the gas in their cars. Doctors could not access the medical records of their patients and diagnostic tests could not be performed on the critically ill. Emergency response systems could not function. The entire nation experienced a cyber blackout that disrupted the political, economic, social, and military operations of the country.

This fictional attack would have affected not only the target state, but also millions of people around the world who would be caught in the crossfire as casualties of this cyber blockade. With cyber access now a necessity in daily life, disruptions can have major consequences. Many people think of cyberspace as information transmitted freely over the airwaves, independent of geography and physical infrastructure, but the reality is much different. Cyberspace is territorially based with a physical web or infrastructure that can be manipulated to deter or punish adversaries, be they states, corporations, or individuals.

The information age of the twenty-first century is distinguished by the proliferation of networks of power that transmit information in a variety of forms and have the effect of defining and decentralizing power relationships. The instantaneous transmission of information through vast geographic space has made our current global economic system possible, as it has the operations of modern governments, militaries, and social organizations. Their capabilities hinge on the accessibility of cyberspace to all participants. To be absent from these networks of information is to be absent from power.[1]

Cyberspace is a physical domain created by the information systems that enable electronic interactions to occur.[2] It supports a wide range of activities throughout the information infrastructure of society and government institutions and creates a distinct new environment. An often overlooked fact is that the domain of cyberspace and its terrain are partially (but not entirely) man-made for the purpose of creation, transmittal, and use of information.[3] Human activity in this environment requires conscious direction and employment of energy, and nothing will happen in the environment without human initiative. As a result of its man-made character-istics, the environment for cyber warfare is more mutable than other domains, whereas actions that corrupt, disrupt, or destroy the components of digital information networks have the potential to change the landscape of cyberspace.[4] It is a physical web of connections that can be manipulated to deter or punish adversaries.

Cyber attacks and cyber warfare have received significant attention in recent years because of the threat they pose to security in both the public and private sectors. Cyber attacks are happening on a regular basis: major institutions in the United States and around the world are being targeted for information on diplomatic, security, and financial affairs.[5] Just a few decades ago, attacks on cyberspace would have been mere inconveniences, but because of the nation's ever-expanding dependency on cyberspace, isolation, corruption, or elimination of access to cyberspace could bring life as we know it to a halt. Given the reliance on cyberspace, it "has arguably become a center of gravity not just for military operations, but for *all* aspects of national activity, to include economic operations, diplomatic, and other transactions."[6] Part of the devastation of the September 11, 2001, attacks on the World Trade Center and other targets was that al-Qaeda attempted to destroy a hub of international commercial activity, which was linked to global markets via cyberspace. Opponents of advanced capitalism or modern societies can seek to attack arenas where cyberspace is a crucial element of commerce.

As best we know, cyber attacks have not yet directly resulted in deaths, but they do disrupt vital services that would damage productivity, economic growth, and national security. In 2008, estimated losses to industry due to intellectual property and theft in cyberspace ranged as high as $1 trillion.[7] Every year, hackers break into US government systems, corporations, and research institutions and steal tens of billions of dollars in the form of intellectual property, technology, and trade secrets.[8]

There are four important components of information infrastructure: physical facilities and equipment; software and standards; information resources; and people. There are also three major types of attack in cyberspace: mechanical attacks (i.e., bombing of command-and-control centers), electromagnetic attacks (i.e., electromagnetic pulses), and digital attacks (i.e., intrusion of systems and networks).[9]

Attacks in cyberspace can be either tactical or strategic.[10] Much of cyber security research focuses on the tactical threats—attacks on individuals or small groups, hackers, and corporate or government espionage. Yet, because cyberspace is the primary medium for communication of a range of types of data in the global international system, there remains the potential for strategic cyber attacks. Strategic attacks in cyberspace include the ability of an actor to deny use of cyberspace to states. Actors who can control another's access to cyberspace can seriously damage the economy, military readiness, social organizations, and political legitimacy of a state. The longer access can be denied or controlled, the more damage can be rendered.[11]

Despite cyberspace comprising a global web of interconnectedness, countries and regions can still be excluded or cut off from cyberspace without the rest of the world experiencing a marked reduction in capabilities.[12] Some countries have experienced degradation of cyberspace access due to accidental damage of the critical physical infrastructure that supports it: In 2008, three undersea fiber-optic cables were accidentally damaged, resulting in disruption of cyberspace access to parts of the Middle East and Asia. During this time, Egypt temporarily lost approximately 55 percent of its access to the internet (the internet is a major component of cyberspace).[13] Other countries have lost cyber access to major institutions, such as banks and government offices, due to cyber attacks. In April 2009, ten fiber-optic cables were cut in California, all located within easy access of manhole covers. In several cases, the backup cables that ran next to the primary cables were also cut, resulting in tens of thousands of citizens being unable to access land and mobile telephone services, including emergency response services, police, and hospitals.[14]

Estonia and Georgia experienced debilitating cyber attacks in 2007 and 2008, respectively, which took down key government and financial websites. At least one country has chosen to "turn off" its connection to cyberspace in order to preserve the integrity of the internal, domestic web when under attack: In response to cyber attacks on its system, Estonia turned off its connection to external cyber networks in 2007. Others states, such as Iran, China, Burma, Egypt, and Syria, have restricted cyber communication during periods of domestic turbulence. These actions can have serious implications. According to the Organization for Economic Cooperation and Development, the Egyptian economy lost an estimated $18 million per day, for a total of $90 million over five days, when the Mubarak regime shut down access to the internet in an effort to quell domestic unrest in January 2011.[15]

All of this suggests that cyberspace can be "turned off" or rendered inaccessible intentionally and unintentionally by actors who are internal or external to the country.[16] The idea that individuals, small groups, or states can intentionally shut down cyberspace poses a serious quandary to all who rely on cyberspace for essential activities. An act that would have such deleterious consequences for an entire state merits serious study of the conditions under which something like this could be possible and how it might be prevented.

Goals of the Book

The purpose of this book is to understand how these types of attacks could shut down, close off, or otherwise render cyberspace useless for an entire country. What if access to cyberspace could be denied at will? What would be the implications? The goals of this research are to develop an understanding of what a cyber blockade is, when it might be used, and how it might affect the security of states and other actors, and the implications for scholarship and policy.

Blockades in cyberspace are an emergent tool in the panoply of international relations. Cyber blockade is a situation rendered by an attack on cyber infrastructure or systems that prevents a state from accessing cyberspace, thus preventing the transmission (ingress and egress) of data beyond a geographical boundary. Cyber blockades carry the potential to inflict political, economic, military, and social damage on the target state, and can be considered acts of war.

In developing a cyber strategy, states must consider the implications of blockades in cyberspace, including how to use them and how to defend against them. The *Tallinn Manual on the International Law Applicable to Cyber Warfare*, the prominent international effort to determine how existing international laws of armed conflict apply to cyberspace, addressed the concept of cyber blockades but ultimately failed to achieve consensus among the experts regarding the existence, establishment, and enforcement of cyber blockades.[17]

These types of attacks are politically and economically damaging forms of warfare, yet we do not understand much about them, in part because we lack a theory to inform our use of or defense against them. They pose significant questions regarding legality, the role of state and nonstate actors, and the nature of conflict for national security and the international community. Theories related to cyber warfare, including the lack of a theory for blockade in cyberspace, are still in the earliest stages of development, yet cyber security is an important problem that needs to be examined urgently and systematically.

As stated in the White House's *International Strategy for Cyberspace*, "long-standing international norms guiding state behavior—in times of peace and conflict—also apply in cyberspace. Nonetheless, unique attributes of networked technology require additional work to clarify how these norms apply and what additional understandings might be necessary to supplement them."[18] The goals of this book are to develop a theory of blockades in cyberspace by expanding upon and updating the literature on blockades as it relates to cyberspace.

The two main questions of this research seek to define cyber blockades and understand the conditions under which they are likely to occur. The first question is: What are cyber blockades, including their structures and components? To answer this, we must establish how a cyber blockade differs from a traditional blockade and how it is similar. We also need to develop an understanding of the actors involved in cyber blockades, resources necessary to establish cyber blockades, how they are conducted, and the potential effects of these operations.

The second question is: Why do actors use cyber blockades as a tool of international relations? To shed light on the answer, we must investigate the role of anonymity and plausible deniability in these types of attacks, the international legal status of cyber blockades, and any conditions that could make a state more vulnerable to cyber blockades. In addition, we must address the alternative options for actors considering implementing a cyber blockade.

Case Studies

The two cases of Estonia and Georgia are intrinsically important because they are arguably the only two cases of cyber warfare in history. Even though the definition of cyber warfare is controversial, both cases involve nation-states that called upon military action in response to cyber attacks.[19] Thus, while this research uses a case study approach, the cases selected comprise the current universe of cyber warfare.[20] In addition, the case selection provides variance on the type of actors involved, including states, nonstate actors, and the private sector. Finally, the conditions under which the attacks occurred are different because one was part of a military operation and the other was not.

Definition of Cyberspace and Key Terms

This book defines a cyber blockade as the situation rendered by an attack on cyber infrastructure or systems that prevents a state from accessing cyberspace, thus preventing the transmission (ingress and egress) of data beyond a geographical boundary. A cyber blockade differs from censorship or other forms of domestic control that occur when a government prevents its own population from receiving or transmitting certain information, usually for reasons of internal stability. The cyber blockade must be effective in preventing the transmission of information; the duration of the blockade is a secondary consideration that matters in terms of generating the desired effect. A cyber blockade that lasts for only a split second would have such little impact that it would not matter; however, a blockade timed to coincide with a critical date (such as an election day) or one that is sustained for several weeks or months could both be considered effective, depending on the goals of the blockade. Just as with naval blockades, maintaining the blockade for a specific, predetermined period of time is not an essential part of the blockade; it is the blockade's effectiveness at achieving its goals that matters most.

There are many definitions of cyberspace. The best definition for the purposes of this research is "a global domain within the information environment whose distinctive and unique character is framed by the use of electronics and the electromagnetic spectrum to create, store, modify, exchange, and exploit information via interdependent and interconnected networks using information-communication technology."[21] Cyberspace is a physical domain and not an entirely man-made environment because it involves physical elements and properties that exist independent of cyberspace (such as properties of mathematics and physics) and cuts across other domains (e.g., land, sea, and air) that are not man-made. Essentially, it is a partially man-made environment that consists of physical attributes (such as computers and cables) as well as digital attributes (such as bits and bytes of data) and uses information technology to manage information passed along networks that create a web of connections and interdependence.

The *terrain* in cyberspace (not the whole domain) is almost completely man-made for the creation, transmittal, and use of information. Thus, the man-made aspects of the environment are mutable and changes in components of digital information networks transform the shape of cyberspace.[22] Cyberspace is the "place" where digital data flows and computer-mediated communication occurs; this includes but is not limited to the internet or its cables.

Cyber power can be defined as "the ability to use cyberspace to create advantages and influence events in all the operational environments and across the instruments of power."[23] Cyber power, just like power in international relations (IR) theory, is a multifaceted concept that is "complex, indeterminate, and intangible," as Peter L. Hays wrote.[24] It includes the possession of capabilities to conduct military and other operations in and through cyberspace, utilizing the medium for commercial or other peaceful purposes, as well as warfare. Cyberspace and cyber power broadened traditional IR theory to include new aspects that bridge the space-and-time continuum that is a defining feature of other domains and move beyond traditional horizontal geographic configurations to include vertical dimension that extends through airwaves and satellite transmissions.

Cyber warfare, like other types of warfare, has many definitions. The United Nations does not have a definition of cyber warfare, but other historical definitions of warfare may be applicable.[25] Cyber warfare can be thought of as Clausewitz famously described as "the continuation of politics by other means."[26] In *On War*, Clausewitz also described war as "nothing but a duel on an extensive scale . . . an act of violence to compel our opponent to fulfill our will."[27] A Sun Tzu-inspired definition describes cyber warfare as "the art and science of fighting without fighting; of defeating an opponent without spilling their blood."[28] At its most basic level, cyber warfare is a state of hostilities between countries or their agents (including organized nonstate groups under the control of the state) that involves cyber operations that result in damage, destruction, or death.

Cyber attack is defined as "deliberate actions to alter, disrupt, deceive, degrade, or destroy computer systems or networks or the information and/or programs resident in or transiting these systems or networks."[29] NATO's *Tallinn Manual* stipulates that an attack in cyberspace must result in damage, destruction, or death in order to qualify as an armed attack under international law.[30] Cyber attacks contrast with cyber exploitation, which is the surreptitiously obtained confidential information via cyberspace and includes a range of actions from official government spying to corporate espionage to individual-level identity theft.

Outline of the Book

The rest of this book deals directly with the issue of blockades and cyber blockades. The next chapter presents an overview of the unique features of cyberspace and how it fits with traditional theories of international relations. The third chapter presents an analysis of blockades in four domains: land, sea, air, and space. The purpose of this analysis is to highlight commonalities and differences among a variety of types of blockades and assess which features are most likely to apply in cyberspace. The fourth chapter presents a case study of the cyber attacks on Estonia in 2007, the first case of cyber blockade and arguably the first cyber war. The fifth chapter discusses the cyber attacks on Georgia during the Georgian-Russian War of 2008, a war that represented the first time cyber attacks were combined with traditional military operations. The sixth chapter provides an analysis of the blockade operations in cyberspace and compares them to blockades in other domains. It seeks to answer how the two cases of cyber blockades compare with each other and with other types of blockades. Finally, the last chapter provides recommendations to scholars and policymakers who are confronting challenges related to cyber blockades and similar types of operations.

Notes

1. Castells, *Communication Power*.
2. Rattray, *Strategic Warfare in Cyberspace*. For a list of some of the many definitions of cyberspace, see Table 2-1 Definitions of Cyberspace, in Kuehl, "From Cyberspace to Cyberpower: Defining the Problem," 26–27.
3. Rattray, *Strategic Warfare in Cyberspace*.
4. Ibid., 65.
5. Baker and Waterman, "In the Crossfire: Critical Infrastructure in the Age of Cyber War."
6. Lambeth, "Airpower, Spacepower, and Cyberpower," in *Toward a Theory of Cyberpower*, ed. Lutes and Hays, 166.
7. Andress, Winterfeld, and Rogers, *Cyber Warfare: Techniques, Tactics and Tools for Security Practitioners*, 8.
8. Nakashima, "U.S. Said to Be Target of Massive Cyber-Espionage Campaign."
9. Rattray, *Strategic Warfare in Cyberspace*, 17–32.
10. Clausewitz defines tactics as the use of armed forces in engagements, and strategy as the use of engagements for the objective of war, according to Martel, *Victory in War: Foundations of Modern Strategy*, 37. For a lengthier discussion of the evolution of the definitions of strategy and tactics, see ibid. For a discussion of strategy and tactics in cyberspace, see Lewis, "Thresholds for Cyber War."
11. The damage inflicted by cyber attacks is difficult to quantify because it involves lost economic productivity, degraded political and military capabilities, and psychological effects, such as fear. Experts have estimated that a five-day shutdown of the internet in

Egypt cost approximately $18 million per day. Experts also estimate that serious cyber attacks (not complete shutdowns) cost approximately $6.3 million per day. See Schwartz, "Egypt Takes $90 Million Hit from Internet Blackout"; Baker and Waterman, "In the Crossfire: Critical Infrastructure in the Age of Cyber War."

12. Because the internet is a "web," by definition it creates multiple pathways between and among nodes. One of the key strengths of the web is that it is designed to have inherent redundancies and alternative pathways to transmit information.

13. Johnson, "Faulty Cable Blacks Out Internet for Millions"; and Associated Press, "Third Internet Cable Cut in the Middle East."

14. Andress, Winterfeld, and Rogers, *Cyber Warfare: Techniques, Tactics and Tools for Security Practitioners*, 133.

15. Schwartz, "Egypt Takes $90 Million Hit from Internet Blackout."

16. The internet is a part of cyberspace. The internet is "a collective noun for thousands of smaller networks, run by corporations, governments, universities and private businesses, all stitched together to form one (mostly) seamless, global, 'internetworked' whole. In theory, the internet is meant to be widely distributed and heavily resilient, with many possible routes between any two destinations. In practice, a combination of economics and geography means that much of its infrastructure is concentrated in a comparatively small number of places." See *Economist*, "Mapping the Tubes."

17. Schmitt, ed. *The Tallinn Manual on the International Law Applicable to Cyber Warfare*, 195–98.

18. The White House, "International Strategy for Cyberspace."

19. Andress, Winterfeld, and Rogers, *Cyber Warfare: Techniques, Tactics and Tools for Security Practitioners*, 12.

20. It was mentioned earlier that states have not agreed on a set of criteria for cyber warfare, but the cases of Georgia and Estonia are the two most frequently cited cases of cyber warfare to date. Cyber warfare itself is a disputed term. Consistent with Carl von Clausewitz's understanding of warfare, scholars such as Thomas Rid argue that the use of force in war must be violent, instrumental, and political. The Tallinn Manual stipulates that an attack in cyberspace must result in damage, destruction, or death in order to qualify as an armed attack, and thus an act of war, under international law. Michael Schmitt presents a framework for cyber war: Cyber attacks must surpass certain thresholds for severity, immediacy, directness, invasiveness, measurability, presumptive legitimacy, and responsibility in order to be considered warfare. In 2011, the US Department of Defense did not directly define cyber war, but stated that the War Powers Act would apply to a situation that brought about "the introduction of United States Armed Forces into hostilities or into situations where imminent involvement in hostilities is clearly indicated by the circumstances, and to the continued use of such forces in hostilities or in such situations." For more information, see Rid, *Cyber War Will Not Take Place*; Schmitt, *The Tallinn Manual on the International Law Applicable to Cyber Warfare*; Franklin D. Kramer, Stuart H. Starr, and Larry K. Wentz, *Cyberpower and National Security*, 1st ed. (Washington, DC: National Defense University Press; Potomac Books, 2009); and US Department of Defense, "Department of Defense Cyberspace Policy Report" (November 2011).

21. Kuehl, "From Cyberspace to Cyberpower: Defining the Problem," 28.

22. Rattray, *Strategic Warfare in Cyberspace*, 65.

23. Kuehl, "From Cyberspace to Cyberpower: Defining the Problem," 38.

24. Pfaltzgraff, "International Relations Theory and Spacepower," on page 41, quoting Hays, *United States Military Space: Into the Twenty-First Century*.

25. Andress, Winterfeld, and Rogers, *Cyber Warfare: Techniques, Tactics and Tools for Security Practitioners*, 3.

26. Clausewitz et al., *On War*; Castells, *Communication Power*.

27. Andress, Winterfeld, and Rogers, on page 3, quoting Clausewitz et al., *On War*.

28. Carr, *Inside Cyber Warfare*, 2.

29. Owens, Dam, and Lin, *Technology, Policy, Law, and Ethics Regarding U.S. Acquisition and Use of Cyberattack Capabilities*, 1.

30. Schmitt, *The Tallinn Manual on the International Law Applicable to Cyber Warfare*.

CHAPTER 2

Theorizing about Cyberspace

Cyberspace as a Commons and a Domain

Cyberspace functions independently of other domains, but it is also a force multiplier that can enhance the power of actions taken in other domains.[1] Dominance in cyberspace can improve the performance of operations in other domains, but the loss of dominance can negate or diminish capabilities in other domains as well. Also, unlike other domains where the blessings of geography have given some states natural advantages over others, there are no natural advantages to any state in the domain of cyberspace; the only advantages are those earned through investment and ingenuity.[2] Furthermore, the cost associated with entry to the cyber domain is remarkably low, especially when compared with entry to the land, sea, air, or space domains. Such low barriers of entry mean that cyberspace can be accessible to virtually anyone, anywhere, at any time.[3]

Cyberspace is unique also because it changes time as a factor in operations; it is characterized by the marked reduction in time, space, distance, and investment for all actors.[4] Cyberspace allows information—and attacks—to travel almost instantaneously across vast distances. These attacks occur much faster than humans can react or respond to them. Theoretical physicist Basarab Nicolescu argues that it would be more accurate to call cyberspace "cyber-space-time" because of the manipulation of time through cyber capabilities. Complexity theory says that cyberspace (or cyber-space-time) is a complex system: one in which numerous independent elements continuously interact and spontaneously organize and reorganize

< 12 >

themselves into more and more elaborate structures over time. According to complexity theory, cyber-space-time is not only chaotic and unknown, but unpredictable as well.[5]

While individual attacks occur quickly across the cyber-space-time continuum, it takes time and resources to innovate and develop the knowledge, software, and systems that will ultimately determine if the attacks are successful. Most sophisticated cyber attacks require significant planning, reconnaissance, and surveillance that occur much slower. A true cyber war would require significant preparation, research, and development time, and it would probably combine the use of cyber weapons with conventional weapons.[6] Knowledge of the physical principles and systems governing the information environment is essential to those who provide security for the domain, in the same way that pilots, sailors, marines, and soldiers require an understanding of the environment in which they conduct warfare and the potential for attacks on its infrastructure.[7]

Because cyberspace provides powerful new technologies, is ubiquitous in other domains, and acts as a force multiplier for traditional military capabilities, defining warfare in cyberspace is problematic. There are a huge number of military and civilian assets at risk worldwide, and cyber technologies have empowered nonstate actors and individuals in unprecedented ways. At the same time, escalation in cyberspace is ill-defined, the threshold for physical action or retaliation is unclear, and there is no consensus on appropriate targets for retaliation for cyber attacks.[8] Existing laws and norms are not mature enough to deal with the complexity of cyberspace and its relationship to warfare.[9]

In addition to empowering a diverse array of actors with asymmetrical capabilities, cyberspace also makes attribution extraordinarily difficult, if not impossible. In this context, attribution can be defined as the act of identifying the person or persons responsible for an event. In traditional conflicts, it is relatively easy to know who the enemy is, but this is not the case with cyberspace. For blockades, states were required to announce their intention to blockade another state. Today, states do not announce their actions in cyberspace, there is a proliferation of actors in that domain, and the technology of cyberspace makes it increasingly difficult to determine who is conducting the cyber blockade.

While cyber forensics have become increasingly sophisticated over time, so, too, have attackers. When a cyber attack is in progress, it is difficult for states to assess the scope of the attack and determine who is responsible for it.[10] For most sophisticated cyber aggressors, anonymity or plausible deniability is a major advantage of cyberspace, while it poses a significant challenge to retaliation.[11]

Ultimately, states may be unable to attribute attacks to specific individuals or organizations or link nonstate actors to government sponsors, making it impossible to follow traditional courses of action under international law. Despite this, states may exercise their right of self-defense overtly or covertly by executing counter-cyber measures or other forms of deterrence.[12]

This problem of attribution in cyberspace has also complicated efforts to adapt traditional deterrence strategy to the cyber domain. Traditional deterrence relied on the principles of denial and punishment, but punishment can be an effective deterrent only if the actors believe that the attack will be traced back to the perpetrator. Technological developments have made it increasingly difficult, if not impossible, to have positive attribution for sophisticated cyber attacks.[13] As a result, denial becomes more important when attribution is difficult.[14]

Vulnerabilities in Cyberspace

Cyberspace is similar to traditional domains in that it can be self-contained, but cyberspace differs in that it also traverses other domains. Fiber-optic cables are in the maritime domain, host servers are on land, data passes through air in wireless communications, and the information transmitted and received throughout the cyberspace system is useful for a variety of purposes.[15] There are three different places within the cyberspace domain where geographic or technological chokepoints exist, and they create vulnerabilities for the entire system.

First, the physical infrastructure is vulnerable to attack. While cyberspace is often thought of as a global, wireless entity, its underpinnings are physical. At the most basic level, undersea fiber-optic cables connect continents, and through these cables the transmission and exchange of data occur. Undersea cables lie on the bottom of the ocean, where they are unlikely to be disturbed by operators in the maritime environment. Nevertheless, they are subject to the same geographical constraints as all marine operators: The shortest distance from one place to another is often through a geographical chokepoint, such as a strait or canal. In addition, when the cables reach their destination, they must connect to infrastructure on land. In doing so, they become more vulnerable to disruption (accidental or intentional) as they enter shallow waters and approach landing points. The critical chokepoints are straits or canals and landing points.

Second, "root servers," which direct traffic from one internet protocol (IP) address to another, guide information through the network to its destination. There are thirteen root servers in the world; ten were originally located in the United States, and the other three were originally located in Stockholm, Amsterdam, and Tokyo. Today, nine of the root servers use a routing technique called "anycast" to allow them to operate in multiple geographic locations, making them more secure.[16] In addition, each root server has redundant computer equipment in order to provide reliable service in the event of an attack or a hardware or software failure.

These increased security and redundancy measures were enacted because root servers have been the subject of attacks in the past and are likely to be targets in the future. If these servers cannot function as legitimate and trustworthy operators, then there will be no reliability or trust within the system. Information cannot be reliably transmitted or received, thus compromising the integrity of the system. The impact of an attack on the root servers may be that information cannot be transmitted or received or is seen as untrustworthy.[17] Thus, an attack on the root servers could halt global political and financial transactions until the integrity of the system is reestablished.

Third, computer systems and networks are vulnerable to many different types of attacks. Attacks such as hacking, viruses, and worms are among the most common ways to exploit the vulnerabilities of computer systems and networks. Of particular importance for this book, denial-of-service (DoS) and distributed denial-of-service (DDoS) attacks have the ability to block communications for a wide range of senders and receivers and are relatively easy to execute. Attacks on computer systems and networks can be designed to produce specific effects; they may deny user access to websites or files, destroy stored data files, steal information such as passwords or confidential documents, or lead to the malfunction of physical systems connected to the network.

While they are not part of the geographic or technical chokepoints relevant for blockades, a discussion of cyber security cannot forget the role of users and that individuals are potential vulnerabilities for cyberspace. Malicious actors can deliberately inject destructive scripts or viruses to compromise one or more computer systems. Nonmalicious but corrupt or unethical individuals can be bribed or blackmailed into conducting activities that compromise cyber security. Finally, even well-intentioned, ethical individuals can compromise cyber security through inadvertent, accidental, uninformed, or careless activities that have serious repercussions.

Types of Cyber Attacks

Cyber blockades are the effect or result of cyber attacks, which can be conducted through various means and by various actors. Under the prospective number of means and actors, it is more appropriate to employ an effect-based approach to categorization and classification of cyber attacks. The broad categorization of cyber attacks by effect produces three main categories: theft, denial, and destruction. This approach simplifies the analysis by examining the outcome of the attack, regardless of the perpetrator, affiliations, location, method, and other details.[18]

Cyber theft includes the unlawful and unauthorized seizure of information (to include intellectual property) that belongs to individuals, corporations, or governments. This category ranges from personal identity theft to corporate data hacking to state espionage. These acts are all considered theft because they involve the stealing or unauthorized access of private information or property.

Denial attacks prevent or deny access to information located in cyberspace. These attacks include authorized denial of access to financial information, news and media reporting, and government communications. Denial can be achieved through DoS attacks, which are common and relatively easy to execute, but can have widespread effects. Botnets can take control over computers (making them what is commonly referred to as "zombies") and perpetrate attacks without the legitimate owners' or operators' knowledge or consent. DDoS attacks are often conducted in this manner; a few hackers gain access to other computers, creating zombies and using them to spread malicious codes that overload systems, use all of the available bandwidth, and cause the targeted systems and websites to crash. DoS and DDoS attacks are frequently launched against web servers, mail servers, and other public-facing components of companies or organizations. They can also target the technological components of physical access control systems, transportation systems, or other systems in order to bring them to an abrupt halt.[19] Less commonly, denial attacks can be conducted through physical manipulation of infrastructure or electromagnetic attacks, as discussed below. Denial attacks, particularly DoS and DDoS, are frequent occurrences in cyberspace and are a recurrent problem for information security professionals. Unlike destruction, denial is not permanent but can still have serious effects.

Destruction is the unauthorized defacement or destruction of information and property located in cyberspace or connected to it. This category includes destruction of personal, corporate, or nationally owned information or property and ranges from defacement of corporate websites with political slogans to cyber attacks that manipulate and destroy physical infrastructure, such as nuclear reactors.

Cyber blockades are a type of attack designed to prevent or deny access to cyberspace, which can be achieved through destruction of physical infrastructure or denial attacks. Denial and destruction can occur in many forms and exploit different vulnerabilities. Just as the domain of cyberspace has both natural and man-made elements, attacks in cyberspace can be both natural and man-made and can target either the hardware or the software of cyberspace. Cyber blockades could be constructed using any of three types of attacks that could occur in cyberspace: mechanical or physical attacks, electromagnetic attacks, and digital or virtual attacks.[20]

Physical attacks on hardware and infrastructure require little sophistication or training. Many cables are located in accessible places, such as near manhole covers or buried underground near existing pipelines or railways. Even well-protected government and military facilities are often connected to the public utilities grid, opening them up to increased vulnerabilities and delays in backup systems.[21] Wire cutters or backhoes can cut fiber-optic cables easily and can effectively disrupt service to a large portion of a network. Attacks on physical infrastructure can also target the key network nodes or the power systems that support them, rendering them ineffective. Finally, physical attacks can also target the key personnel who are highly trained to support the networks and responsible for prevention of and recovery after attacks.[22]

Electromagnetic attacks are a rare but powerful form of cyber denial attack. Electromagnetic pulse (EMP) weapons and jamming of transmissions are just two examples of electromagnetic attacks that can cause massive disruptions in service in cyberspace. Of the types of EMP weapons—high-altitude electromagnetic pulse (HAMP) and high-power microwave (HPM)—HPM is probably the likelier threat because it involves the use of nuclear weapons but can be effective on a small scale and with smaller weapons. Furthermore, it is more effective against electronics and more difficult to protect devices against it.[23] Jamming is a type of electronic warfare that can be used to jam devices on the electromagnetic spectrum, including radio, radar, sonar, infrared, laser, and other technologies common in militaries and defense forces.[24]

There are a variety of methods of virtual attacks, such as Web defacement and semantic attacks, domain name server attacks, DDoS or DoS, malicious code (such as the Stuxnet worm), exploitation of routing vulnerabilities, and compound attacks that use multiple methods. DoS and DDoS have special relevance to the concept of blockade in cyberspace. Jose Nazario defines a DDoS attack as "a coordinated effort that instructs PCs [personal computers] to send a victim a flood of traffic designed to overwhelm their systems or consume their bandwidth." The attacks are designed to interrupt the normal flow of traffic to and from the site. Their purpose is to overwhelm an adversary who normally has superior bandwidth resources and operate from a multitude of locations, making it difficult or impossible to filter the traffic.[25] His examination of the politically motivated DDoS attack on Estonia in 2007 and Georgia in 2008 finds that cyber attacks, particularly DDoS and DoS attacks, are simply politics by other means. DDoS attacks can be used as a simple blunt force to silence critics or opponents at home or in foreign countries.[26]

A global survey of government and private industry revealed that cyber attacks, particularly DDoS attacks, are increasingly common and cost millions of dollars for the companies that experience them—an estimated $6.3 million per day for the company under attack. The impacts of attacks on companies and industries are severe and have ramifications that cut across all sectors.[27] It is likely that DDoS and DoS attacks will become more important and pose greater danger to the economy and to politics as the availability of mobile networks increases and becomes more important for the modern information society.[28]

There are ways to defend against physical and virtual attacks in cyberspace and cyberspace technologies. For defense against physical attacks, redundant infrastructure such as cold, warm, and hot backup sites is important, as is facility and equipment hardening such as bomb-proof facilities, gates, guards, and a location that is conducive to such measures. For virtual or digital attacks, software standards and active and passive defense systems are designed to detect and disarm malicious activities. Active defense systems include the National Security Agency's EINSTEIN program, which automatically scans internet traffic for malicious codes and disables them. Passive defense systems include firewalls and antivirus software that keep corrupt or malicious software out of operating systems, but do not necessarily disable or destroy the threats.[29] Finally, information resources and people are the last line of defense in cyberspace. People with the proper training and expertise can take precautionary measures to defend against attacks and recover after them.[30]

In addition, there are many educational and military exercises under way to help mitigate the effects of and plan responses to the myriad world-wide cyber threats. Yet according to reliable sources, there are no exercises designed to see how the US military would operate without access to cyber-space and its enabling capabilities.[31] Cyber blockades would be significantly more damaging if there is no plan of response to this type of attack.

What Constitutes Blockade Operations?

Blockades are a form of anti-access or area-denial operations that can be conducted in many different domains. Historically, they have had a signifi-cant impact on both commerce and military power. Scholars have argued that there are two different but not mutually exclusive types of blockades: naval blockades that prevent the movement of military vessels and com-mercial blockades that target trade.[32] In either case, blockades are tradi-tionally considered acts of war.

International and customary laws define blockades and establish the rules for implementing them. Blockade laws originated in the sixteenth century with the rise in naval power, and these blockades continue today as an important part of wartime operations. The US Navy defines a blockade in the following way:

> Blockade is a belligerent operation to prevent vessels and/or aircraft of all nations, enemy as well as neutral, from entering or exiting specified ports, airfields, or coastal areas belonging to, occupied by or under the control of an enemy nation. While the belligerent right of visit and search is designated to interdict the flow of contraband goods, the belligerent right of blockade is intended to prevent vessels and aircraft, regardless of their cargo, from crossing an established and publicized cordon separating the enemy from international waters and/or airspace.[33]

In laymen's terms, a blockade is "the isolation of a nation, area, city, or harbor by hostile ships or forces in order to prevent the entrance and exit of traffic and commerce."[34] It is a means of physically preventing a country from engaging in the exchange of goods beyond its borders for political reasons and with the intent of weakening the state, government institutions (including the military), economy, or society.[35] The effect of a blockade is to deny access to specific goods and information of value to the adversary; as such, blockades are a type of economic warfare.

Blockades can have many different characteristics. They can be partial or total, limited or unlimited, porous or tight, close (tactical) or distant (strategic). Whatever combination of characteristics blockades assume, the goal is to trap or prevent the free movement of the enemy's military forces and/or commercial trade. The blockading actor must have superior force because he is on the defensive to maintain the blockade.[36]

According to the US naval strategist Alfred Thayer Mahan, the goal of naval blockades is to keep the enemy in port. As he famously stated, "Whatever the number of ships needed to watch those in an enemy's port, they are fewer by far than those that will be required to protect the scattered interests imperiled by an enemy's escape."[37] Mahan also points out that blockades are both offensive and defensive. The offensive characteristics of blockades are "directed against both egress and ingress, but more especially against ingress, being meant to prevent the entrance of needed supplies, and being therefore essentially a blow to communications."[38] The defensive characteristics have as their chief objective "to prevent egress unmolested, because such freedom of issue to an enemy means danger, more or less great, to certain national interests; which, because they lie outside the national boundaries, cannot be protected by ordinary defensive measures."[39]

Blockades are a product of international and customary law, according to which there are five criteria for a blockade. These criteria are relevant for this research because they may provide insights for defining and theorizing about cyber blockades.

1. Establishment: "A blockade must be established by the government of the belligerent nation."[40] The establishment of a blockade is usually accompanied by a declaration from the belligerent nation detailing the date the blockade will begin, its geographical limits, and, if appropriate, the grace period granted to allow neutral vessels to leave the area.[41]

2. Notification: "It is customary for the belligerent nation establishing the blockade to notify all affected nations of its imposition."[42] International law says that notification is obligatory, according to Article 11 of the Declaration of London in 1909.[43] Neutral vessels and aircraft are entitled to notification so that they can avoid the

blockaded area. In addition, the local authorities in the blockaded areas must also be notified, but the form of notification does not matter, as long as it is effective.[44]

3. Effectiveness: "To be valid, a blockade must be effective." It can be maintained by force or other means, as long as ingress and egress of the blockaded area are sufficiently impeded.[45] The use of a particular type of weapon or enforcement mechanism is not required as long as the blockade is effective. Effectiveness does not require that every avenue of approach to the area be covered, just sufficient lines of approach so that ingress or egress is either not possible or dangerous.[46]

4. Impartiality: "A blockade must be applied impartially to the vessels and aircraft of all nations."[47] Belligerent forces are not permitted to discriminate among the vessels or aircraft based on their country of origin because the goal of the blockade is to prevent trade with the blockaded state. However, belligerent forces can discriminate based on the type of vessel (commercial, military, or private civilian) or goods that it is carrying (e.g., oil or weapons) and still operate within this criterion.[48]

5. Limitations: A blockade must not bar access to or departure from neutral ports and coasts, and it must not interfere with trade or communications that do not involve the blockaded area. Neutral states maintain the right to trade with neutral states, and a blockading force cannot interfere with the trade among neutrals. In addition, a blockade is prohibited if its sole purpose is to starve the civilian population or deny it access to goods essential for survival.[49]

Pacific blockades are similar to the blockades described above, but with one notable exception: In a pacific blockade, the blockading state does not purport to bring about a state of war. Pacific blockades cut off access to or egress from ports or coasts by naval operations and are "designed to compel the territorial sovereign to yield to demands made of it, such as the granting of redress for the consequences of its wrongful conduct."[50] These blockades are pacific in that the blockading power is disposed to remain at peace, and the blockaded entity can decide to treat the blockade as an operation that does not compel it to declare war.[51] Thus, pacific blockades can be useful means of gaining redress without resorting to war.[52]

Economic Warfare

Blockades are often, but not always, a means of economic warfare. Economic competition among states is important because economic resources provided the financial means for actors to build military capacity and invest in defense or war-making capabilities that would allow them to protect their gains and prospectively increase their wealth. As a result, wealth is viewed as a symbol of status and power.

In the competition between actors, whether empires, city-states, or nations, control over economic resources has a direct impact on war-making ability. According to Knorr, "historically viewed, economic warfare has been practiced with considerable frequency, although usually by means of military operations."[53] The rational objective of economic warfare in non-zero-sum conflicts should not be to cause an absolute maximum loss in the enemy's economic capability, but rather to cause a relative loss in the enemy's economic capability and minimize damage to one's own economy.[54] In zero-sum conflicts, absolute maximum loss to the enemy's capabilities may be desirable.

Economic warfare was defined by Yuan-li Wu in 1952:

> The concept of economic warfare may be interpreted in two different ways. In a narrow sense, it refers to all those international economic measures which directly enhance a country's relative strength. These measures are to be taken primarily, though not exclusively, *during a military conflict* [emphasis added] in order to supplement other forms of warfare. In a broad sense, it comprises all those foreign economic policies that may have as their long-run objective the enlargement of a country's sphere of economic influence (and possibly a consequent contraction of that of a potential adversary).[55]

In centuries past, economic power was closely linked to seapower. Seapower enabled states to exchange goods and information on a global scale. The greater the volume of imports and exports, the greater the state's economic capacity. A state's ability to raise money and maintain sea-based networks around the world was linked to its ability to wage war. Thus, in the age of seapower, establishing command of the seas and control over strategic lines of communication was essential to promoting commerce and building military power.[56] The capability to deny an opponent access to the sea through the implementation of a naval blockade was a significant source of power. Today, the capability to deny an opponent access to cyberspace is one of the most potent sources of power in economic warfare.

Theoretical Grounding in International Relations

International relations (IR) theory traditionally focuses on the concepts of war and peace and conflict and cooperation in the world system and the arrangement of political units within that system. Traditionally, the primary units of international relations have been states or other political entities that control physical territory and resources. Increasingly in the twentieth and twenty-first centuries, nonstate actors have risen to prominence within the international system.

IR theories seek to describe or prescribe interactions and relationships in the international system. Cyberspace is an area of growing importance in which these theories about political units and interactions can be tested and applied. IR theories can help scholars and policymakers understand how cyberspace affects the relationships between political units and how political units affect cyberspace. In particular, cyberspace empowers nonstate actors with unprecedented asymmetric capabilities; thus the IR theories that discuss the role of nonstate actors have direct relevance. Given that cyberspace is a relatively new domain and we have less experience with it than with other domains, extrapolation from IR theories is necessary to help us understand relationships in cyberspace.[57]

The international relations literature supports the question of cyber blockades with four contending theories of politics that attempt to explain conflict and cooperation in the world. Cyberspace is a global forum for cooperation, collaboration, and conflict across the time-and-space continuum, whereas blockades represent a method of warfare employed during times of serious conflict and warfare. Thus, this research must examine themes of both cooperation and conflict and the major IR theories that seek to explain them: geography and technology; realism; liberalism; and constructivism.

The Roles of Geography and Technology

Political behavior is affected by the milieu—the social, political, cultural, and geographic environment in which actors exist. Geography influences decision making in world politics in profound ways, but technology has helped to create new geostrategic relationships that are not limited by the realities of geography. Technology, from the sailing ship to the nuclear-powered submarine, or the propeller aircraft to the long-range bomber, has changed actors' relationships with geography and with each other.

The US naval strategist Alfred Thayer Mahan believed that the technology of seapower permitted power projection on a global scale for the first time and created new economic and military relationships that traversed the globe and increased state power. British geostrategist Sir Halford Mackinder saw that the development of the railroad opened vast expanses of landmasses to the rapid transportation of goods and people, bringing previously isolated regions into contact with major trade routes and cities. The Italian air power theorist Giulio Douhet pointed out that the technology of airpower changed the nature of warfare by expanding the capacity for power projection beyond the sea.[58]

In the twentieth century, technology of space exploration and intercontinental ballistic missiles opened outer space to human influence and created a new set of geographic factors for consideration in the understanding of state power. In the twenty-first century, communications power has reduced the time-and-space relationship between different parts of the globe to the point where communication is virtually instantaneous. This new communications technology has once again transformed our understanding of the relevance of geography and introduced a new set of environmental factors that affect the relationships between and among states.[59]

Realism

Power is the key concept in classical realist theory by which states seek to maintain, increase, or demonstrate their power. Realist theory posits that the international system is based on the assumptions that states are key actors; international politics is inherently conflictual; the struggle for power takes place in an anarchical setting; and states must rely on methods of self-help. In this environment, states are rational, sovereign actors with a variety of capabilities.[60]

Neorealism acknowledges the importance of power but posits that structural factors of the international system, such as anarchy and the distribution of power within the system, are the key concepts for understanding international relations. According to this theory, states seek to preserve or increase their power and standing in the world system, which they can do only through increased capabilities. The increase in capabilities creates a change in the balance of power in the international system, allowing some states to achieve more security while making others less secure. This drive for increased power and capabilities is essential in the international system because only power can ensure the survival of the state.[61] Neorealism seeks to clarify how states choose to use their capabilities and how they are ranked in the system according to their capabilities.[62]

Neoclassical realism states that the anarchical system exists and security within it fluctuates based on material factors. In this system, all types of power, including military and economic, matter in the pursuit of state interests. State behavior, which is guided by self-preservation, is shaped by international interactions and the domestic-level material factors that influence security, such as technology, geography, economics, and support for international institutions. These material factors affect domestic-level decision making by shaping the options and limits of a state's power. Thus, state actions and capabilities can impact the state's position within the international system as well as the system as a whole.

A theory of cyber blockades fits into the tradition of realism because blockades traditionally have been a type of state military capability and cyberspace is a new or burgeoning capability for many states. These capabilities may affect a state's ability to survive in an anarchical, self-help environment and may shape decision making regarding states' options and limitations as well as the balance of power in the international system.

Liberalism

Liberalism is the grand theory that contends with realism to explain the international system. It is based on the idea that there exists a harmony of interest among states and that cooperation will help states achieve their goals better than competition alone can. Cooperation can be furthered by the establishment of institutions that bring together epistemic communities to address particular issues and engage in the creation of regulations or norms.[63]

Liberalism treats integration as a process that involves both high and low politics and actors with both technical expertise and political goals. Neofunctionalists argue that cooperation in one area will engender greater cooperation overall through the process of spillover to other actors and other specializations. Gradually, technical cooperation will lead to political cooperation. Joseph Nye identifies the mechanisms for this process and its integrative potential. The mechanisms include spillover, rising transaction, linkages among different institutions, elite socialization to the concept, regional group formation, ideological and identitive appeal, and the involvement of external actors. The integrative potential lies in the symmetry or economic equality of the units, complementary elite values, economic pluralism, and capacity of states to adapt and respond differently.[64]

Integration theories also address the basis for international collaborative structures and processes that hold immediate relevance in an integrated, networked world. The integration literature favors the idea that as countries and societies become more interdependent, there will be less armed conflict and military power will play a less important role in world affairs. These theories posit that as states have intertwined their economies to an unprecedented degree, they have reduced some of their independent economic capacities in order to be more efficient within the global system. The economic interdependence of states has reduced incentives and increased costs for a belligerent to make war on its neighbor.

Cyberspace and its associated technologies have allowed countries to become more intertwined than ever before. Cyberspace helps form connections within high and low politics and helps bridge both of them. It provides a forum for the exchange of ideas that facilitates Nye's integrative process and aids with the building of epistemic communities and international collaborative structures that integrationists believe will reduce conflict in the world.

One consequence of integration, however, is that it may have also opened up new areas of vulnerability. The intertwinements of economics that have allowed states to become more efficient have made them more dependent on each other and more vulnerable to an attack on a key node within the network or on the system itself. In achieving greater interdependence and efficiency, states sacrificed some economic production and self-sufficiency, which also means they reduced their sovereignty. In addition, the intertwinement of state-level economies does not necessarily mean that there will be a reduction in conflict, but rather that conflict may shift to include newly empowered actors, such as individuals and nonstate actors who have greater access to information and new types of power in an interconnected world.

INFORMATION SOCIETY AND THE POWER OF COMMUNICATION

In the twenty-first century, the world is more interconnected and interdependent than ever before. The "spillover" that was novel at the end of World

War II has now taken on a life of its own, assisted by the creation of new technologies that allow individuals and organizations to communicate, collaborate, and cooperate in unprecedented ways. According to integration theories, these technologies that connect actors are also likely to reduce the chance of conflict, since conflict would be more likely to negatively affect both sides. However, recent theories such as the "black swan" theory argue that the increased complexity created by interconnectedness may be producing overall instability that is difficult to forecast.[65]

Power remains important in the twenty-first century, but power can be defined differently—more broadly—from the way that it is traditionally viewed in realist theory. Power relations take on spatiotemporal formations that exist throughout society, creating the "network society" that is defined by nodes of power and interconnected communications.[66] Communication depends on the flow of information from communication networks for their origin and diffusion.[67] Interdisciplinary scholar Manuel Castells describes the "space of flows" as the place where electronic information flows in and out of distant nodes in a series of synchronized, real-time interactions. As such, it is a new spatial-temporal organization that has developed under a new technological paradigm.[68]

According to Castells, the most fundamental form of power lies in the ability to shape the human mind, which can be achieved through mastering and manipulating the flow of information on networks. According to Castells, "in the network society, discourses are generated, diffused, fought over, internalized, and ultimately embodied in human action, in the socialized communications realm constructed around local-global networks of multi-modal, digital communication, including the media and the Internet. Power in the network society is communication power."[69]

Castells points out that in this networked society, the holders of power are the networks of actors who exercise power in their respective areas of influence through the networks that they construct around their interests. Switching between and among different networks is a fundamental source of power because it links together meanings and ideas from different networks.[70] According to Castells, the autonomous construction of meaning can only continue in the future by preserving the global commons of communication networks, which are made possible today by the internet. Thus, "there is a fundamental form of exercising power that is common to all networks: exclusion from the network."[71] Because networks are global, exclusion from the network society is a pervasive source of power.

NETWORKS AND CONFLICT

Network analysis challenges traditional views of power in international relations by redefining power as the actor's position within the network and the persistent relationships associated with that position. The actors involved in cyber blockades are likely to come from different levels of analysis and be embedded within networks of power. Understanding how networks change the historical discussion of actors, power, and influence is an important step in understanding how and why cyber blockades can occur.

According to Hafner-Burton, Kahler, and Montgomery, two characteristics of networks are particularly important in international relations: the ability of actors to increase their power by exploiting or enhancing their positions within networks and the fungibility of network power. Networks often comprise many levels of analysis (e.g., states, transnational actors, nonstate actors, and individuals) simultaneously operating within one network.[72]

In the twenty-first century, society has reorganized away from vertical, hierarchical organizations and toward horizontal networks.[73] Networks can be organized or harnessed for many different purposes, including nefarious purposes. Oppositional or "dark" networks create problems and disorder within the world (such as drug trafficking or terrorism). These dark networks create "wicked" problems, but other networks can help address these types of problems.[74]

Networked organizational structures mean that groups of individuals can come together quickly, or swarm, to attack without a leader or formal leadership structure. This type of networked warfare, or "netwar," is a "lower-intensity, societal-level counterpart" than the traditional concept of military cyberwar.[75] John Arquilla and David Ronfeldt argue that networked organizations have reinvigorated older forms of licit and illicit activity that may pose serious risks to actors such as militaries and governments that do not recognize and quickly adapt to these new threats presented by nonstate actors.[76]

This new organization of society into networks has led to what Mary Kaldor describes as "new wars." The new wars of the modern era differ in important ways from the "old wars" of the past several centuries. A defining feature of the new wars is the proliferation of nonstate actors who are local and global as well as public and private. New wars blur the boundaries of traditional war, organized crime, and violations of human rights and frequently employ tactics that are outside of international law.[77]

Van Creveld posits that five key issues are important to understanding the recent changes in warfare, which he calls hybrid warfare: the proliferation of actors involved; relationships between the actors; strategies and tactics employed; the goal of the conflict; and the motivations for the individual soldiers.[78] Together, Kaldor and Van Creveld provide a framework that can guide our understanding of the evolving nature of new wars or hybrid warfare in a networked society and the cyber domain.

Constructivism

The constructivist approach to IR theory provides fertile ground for discussions of cyberspace. While most IR theories focus on power and the structure of the relationships between and among units in the international system, constructivism is an ontology focused on the way that meaning is created in the world. Constructivism seeks to bring about an understanding of the way the world is constantly being "constructed" (and reconstructed) on the basis of political, economic, and strategic changes and how these changes are affecting political, social, and economic affairs in the world. Constructivism posits that all human affairs are ultimately social interactions that are defined by the arrangement of the individuals or groups in the system, who have free will to determine what constitutes socially acceptable and unacceptable behavior.[79]

For cyberspace, constructivism means that the actors have the ability to create the arrangements for cyberspace that they wish, including codes of conduct, laws, rules, and norms. This process for creating an arrangement for interactions within cyberspace is the formation of an intersubjective consensus that arises through thoughtful discussion and action. Thus, with cyberspace we have the opportunity to construct an understanding of behaviors, actions, and institutions that we can translate into a reality of rules and institutions.[80]

Uniquely, cyberspace is the medium for the creation of an intersubjective consensus about itself as well as other political, economic, and social issues. As a medium for transmission of data and information, cyberspace enables individuals and groups to engage in the discussions that form the basis for common understanding of all social, political, and economic behaviors. As Manuel Castells and many constructivists have argued, this creation of meaning is the basis for power and relationships in the world. To put it another way, the technological function of cyberspace enables the sharing of ideas and the creation of meanings, expectations, and values that impact strategic thinking and theorizing across a broad spectrum of political, economic, and social issues that impact all actors. This social construction of rules and norms affects and sometimes defines political and social relationships among political units within and beyond cyberspace.

Conclusion

Research indicates that the threat of massive cyber attacks will continue to rise as the world becomes increasingly reliant on cyberspace for essential activities. Just as sea lanes were the highways of world commerce in the age of seapower, cyberspace is the medium for electronic transmission of a significant portion of world commerce, financial investments, government operations, and social communications today.[81] We may not recognize cyber blockades as frequent in the world today, but they are likely to become so in the future.

The theories of IR help explain the role of technology as a tool for conflict and cooperation in world politics and how power is conceptualized in an interconnected environment. Technology, geography, and international politics are inextricably linked. Realism emphasizes the importance of power for states, as measured by capabilities, in the self-help system, whereas liberalism underscores the potential for cooperation in an increasingly globalized and interconnected world. Constructivism demonstrates how information technology has already and will continue to shape our understanding of the environment and influence the course of world politics.

The literature on cyberspace does not directly address the issue of cyber blockades, but there is significant research on related topics, such as the unique attributes of the domain of cyberspace, actors, and vulnerabilities for cyber attacks. The extant literature provides a point of departure for this research project in terms of key issues to be considered in the development of a theory for blockades.

Notes

1. Cyberspace and space are alike in that both are primarily involved in the collection and transmission of information, both pursue functional effects rather than kinetic ones, and both enable operations in the other domains.
2. Lambeth, "Airpower, Spacepower, and Cyberpower," 167–71.
3. Ibid., 167.
4. Ibid.
5. Carr, *Inside Cyber Warfare*, 204–05.

6. Andress, Winterfeld, and Rogers, *Cyber Warfare: Techniques, Tactics and Tools for Security Practitioners*, 170.

7. Rattray, *Strategic Warfare in Cyberspace*, 32.

8. Libicki and Project Air Force (US), *Cyberdeterrence and Cyberwar*, 120.

9. Owens, Dam, and Lin, *Technology, Policy, Law, and Ethics regarding U.S. Acquisition and Use of Cyberattack Capabilities*.

10. Issues complicating the problem of attribution are that the type of attack must be clearly identified (including recognition that it is a deliberate attack, not an unintentional breech), the true location of origin of the attack must be pinpointed, the user associated with that point of origin must be found, the identity of the suspected attacker must be verified, and the role of the attacker (i.e., private individual or government cyber warrior) must be discerned. All of these pieces of information can be difficult to ascertain or impossible to verify, making attribution a serious challenge in cyberspace. For more information, see Brenner, *Cyberthreats: The Emerging Fault Lines of the Nation State*.

11. Glaser, "Deterrence of Cyber Attacks and US National Security"; Libicki and Project Air Force (US), *Cyberdeterrence and Cyberwar*; and Carr, *Inside Cyber Warfare*, 45.

12. Carr, *Inside Cyber Warfare*, 282.

13. Libicki and Project Air Force (US), *Cyberdeterrence and Cyberwar*.

14. Wrenn, "Strategic Cyber Deterrence."

15. Rattray, *Strategic Warfare in Cyberspace*; Owens, Dam, and Lin, *Technology, Policy, Law, and Ethics Regarding U.S. Acquisition and Use of Cyberattack Capabilities*.

16. The other four root servers are located in Maryland and California.

17. In many countries, financial corporations have a legal obligation to cease trading immediately if they receive an indication that the information may not be trustworthy; thus, an attack on the root servers could bring a stop to global financial transactions.

18. Scholars have made many attempts to categorize cyber attacks, but often they result in classifications that are differentiated by details such as location of attack, targets, motivation for attack, identity and affiliations of attacker, and method of attack. These factors are often difficult to determine for many situations and thus are problematic for categorization. Location of attack could be domestic or foreign. Targets may be individuals, corporations, nation-states, or any other actor. Motivation may be financial, political, or ego-related. The identity and affiliation of the attacker helps to differentiate between state/state-sponsored attacks and others. There are various methods of attacks, such as phishing, espionage, or denial of service attacks.

19. Andress, Winterfeld, and Rogers, *Cyber Warfare: Techniques, Tactics and Tools for Security Practitioners*, 176.

20. Rattray, *Strategic Warfare in Cyberspace*, 18.

21. Andress, Winterfeld, and Rogers, *Cyber Warfare: Techniques, Tactics and Tools for Security Practitioners*, 133.

22. Ibid., 128–29.

23. For more details on EMP weapons, see Chapter 6 in Andress, et al., *Cyber Warfare*.

24. Ibid., 129–30.

25. Nazario, "Politically Motivated Denial of Service Attacks"; and Pau, "Business and Social Evaluations of Denial of Service Attacks in View of Scaling Economic Counter-measures."

26. Nazario, "Politcally Motivated Denial of Service Attacks," 179.

27. Baker and Waterman, "In the Crossfire: Critical Infrastructure in the Age of Cyber War."

28. Pau, "Business and Social Evaluations of Denial of Service Attacks in View of Scaling Economic Countermeasures."

29. Andress, Winterfeld, and Rogers, *Cyber Warfare: Techniques, Tactics and Tools for Security Practitioners*, 131–33.

30. Rattray, *Strategic Warfare in Cyberspace*, 32.

31. Andress, Winterfeld, and Rogers, *Cyber Warfare: Techniques, Tactics and Tools for Security Practitioners*, 56.

32. Brodie, *Sea Power in the Machine Age*.

33. US Navy, Marine Corps, and Coast Guard, "The Commander's Handbook on the Law of Naval Operations (Nwp 1-14m, Mcwp 5-12.1, Comdtpub P5800.7a)."

34. *The American Heritage Dictionary of the English Language*.

35. Parmelee, *Blockade and Sea Power: The Blockade, 1914–1919, and Its Significance for a World State*.

36. Mahan, "Blockade in Relation to Naval Strategy," 858; Cdr. Mark D. Hamilton, USN, "Blockade: Why This 19th Century Nelsonian Tool Remains Operationally Relevant Today" (Naval War College, 2007).

37. Mahan, "Blockade in Relation to Naval Strategy," 956.

38. Ibid., 864–65.

39. Ibid., 865.

40. US Navy, "The Commander's Handbook on the Law of Naval Operations."

41. Ibid.

42. Ibid., 7.7.2.2.

43. Oppenheim and Lauterpacht, *International Law: A Treatise*, 874.

44. US Navy, "The Commander's Handbook on the Law of Naval Operations," 7.7.2.2.

45. Ibid., 7.7.2.3.

46. Ibid.

47. Ibid., 7.7.2.4.

48. Ibid.

49. Ibid., 7.7.2.5.

50. Hyde, *International Law, Chiefly as Interpreted and Applied by the United States*, 1667.

51. There are serious objections to pacific blockades on the basis that they interfere with neutrals' rights during times of peace. Ibid., 1671.

52. Ibid., 1668.

53. Knorr, *The Power of Nations: The Political Economy of International Relations*, 139.

54. Ibid., 140.

55. Wu, *Economic Warfare*, 6.

56. Mahan, *The Influence of Sea Power upon History, 1660–1783*.

57. For a similar discussion on the applicability of IR theories to space, see Pfaltzgraff, "International Relations Theory and Spacepower," 37–42.

58. Mahan, *The Influence of Sea Power upon History, 1660–1783*; Mackinder, "The Geographical Pivot of History"; Douhet, *The Command of the Air*.

59. Dougherty and Pfaltzgraff, *Contending Theories of International Relations: A Comprehensive Survey*, 158.

60. Ibid., chapter 2.

61. Mearsheimer, *The Tragedy of Great Power Politics*, chapters 1 and 2.

62. Dougherty and Pfaltzgraff, *Contending Theories of International Relations: A Comprehensive Survey*, chapter 2.

63. Carr and Cox, *The Twenty Years' Crisis, 1919–1939: An Introduction to the Study of International Relations*; Dougherty and Pfaltzgraff, *Contending Theories of International Relations: A Comprehensive Survey*, chapter 10.

64. Nye and Harvard University, *Peace in Parts: Integration and Conflict in Regional Organization*.

65. Taleb, *The Black Swan: The Impact of the Highly Improbable*.

66. Castells, *Communication Power*, 18.

67. Ibid., 431–2.

68. Ibid.

69. Ibid., 53.

70. Ibid., 430.

71. Ibid., 50.

72. Hafner-Burton, Kahler, and Montgomery, "Network Analysis for International Relations."

73. Raab, "Heading toward a Society of Networks: Empirical Developments and Theoretical Challenges."

74. Raab and Milward, "Dark Networks as Problems."

75. Arquilla, Ronfeldt, and US Department of Defense, *Networks and Netwars: The Future of Terror, Crime, and Militancy*, ix.

76. Ibid.

77. Kaldor, *New and Old Wars: Organized Violence in a Global Era*.

78. Van Creveld, *The Transformation of War*.

79. Pfaltzgraff, "International Relations Theory and Spacepower," 53.

80. Dougherty and Pfaltzgraff, *Contending Theories of International Relations: A Comprehensive Survey*, 54.

81. Gerace, *Military Power, Conflict, and Trade*, 29.

CHAPTER 3

Evolution of Blockades in Different Domains

"It is still the custom of old-line military men to talk of blockades and counterblockades as naval strategies, but reality mocks their words."

—Alexander Procofieff De Seversky, *Victory through Air Power*

B lockades occur in different environments and for a variety of reasons; and they are not always called "blockades." It is therefore necessary to look at the full spectrum of blockades in other domains before analyzing recent cyber blockade operations. Blockades are not static; rather, they have evolved significantly over time and with expansion to new domains. Each domain has its own terminology, distinctive physical features, and operating procedures, but whereas every domain is unique, collectively they share a common logic, present a common security environment, and can be mutually supportive of operations in the other domains. Thus, it is important to pursue a common theory of blockades that has specific meaning and application in each domain.[1]

The goal of the chapter is to use this historical understanding as a basis for constructing a preliminary theory of blockades that applies to all domains—land, sea, air, space, and cyberspace. The discussion of cyber blockades is new, but whatever the adjustments are to the new theory, they will be influenced by the history of blockades. As retired Air Vice Marshal Tony Mason of Great Britain's Royal Air Force noted, any truly effective theory of power must emphasize not just the unique characteristics of the instrument, but also "the features it shares, to a greater or lesser degree, with other forms of warfare."[2]

< 34 >

Applicability of Blockades to Cyberspace

In the modern era, information and communication networks are frequently considered goods vital for the economy and national security of almost every country. Communications power is based predominantly in cyberspace and the multitude of networks in it, which could be "turned off" by an enemy. If an adversary could deny access to a significant portion of information and communication of value to the target, this would create the same effect as a blockade—an informational blockade in cyberspace to harm or weaken the adversary by controlling or denying its access to data.

A blockade is commonly thought of as a physical barrier to prevent someone from acquiring something of value in order to gain an advantage. However, a blockade does not need to be physical, as long as it is effective when imposed. Also, blockades are rarely used alone; they are employed as part of a broader strategy to deter and weaken the adversary. Mahan reminds us that the relevant question for blockades is not "does this make it impossible for the enemy to escape?" but "does this impose upon him such risks as to give considerable change of either stopping or crippling him, if he attempts it?"[3]

The forms of blockade have changed dramatically with the evolution of technology, from close blockades to distant blockades to blockade zones, but all have sought the prevention of movement of specific items at, or as close as possible to, their source. As naval scholar Roger Barnett wrote, "States have been rather inventive over the years in conducting blockade operations but calling them something else in order to evade the legal requirements of blockade law."[4] This practice has expanded the idea of the blockade past the strict legal sense to include activities such as quarantines, interceptions, exclusion zones, pacific blockades, and close (tactical) and distant (strategic) blockades. These activities are collectively referred to as *blockade operations*.[5]

In legal terms, however, it is important to distinguish between blockades and zones. Blockades prevent ingress and egress from a particular area (either a state or geographic region within a state). A simple but helpful analogy is a curtain: blockades prevent something (ships, planes, or data) from *traversing* a physical and internationally recognized boundary, but they are not concerned with what happens on the other side of the boundary. In contrast, zones are concerned with what happens *within* a specific geographic area, which may or may not include an international boundary. They are not a dividing line, but a three-dimensional area of exclusion or denial in which the aggressor seeks to control actions.[6] Blockades and zones are two different concepts in terms of international law and as such they have different implications. Most notably, the Law of Armed Conflict requires that blockades be effective and impartial. Zones are not subject to the same requirements, thus are legally easier to manage, but could render a similar amount of damage to the target, particularly in cyberspace.[7]

Despite their differences, popular interpretation conflates blockades and zones. Maritime exclusion zones and no-fly zones are practically synonymous with naval and aerial blockades for so many people, including many practitioners, policymakers, and scholars, that a discussion of blockades that excluded zones would prove unsatisfying to many readers. To address this popular view and simultaneously maintain legal accuracy, this book incorporates research on both blockades and exclusion zones, with the distinctions spelled out above and a promise to revisit these concepts in the final analysis of cyber blockades.

Nonblockade Activities

Before delving into the historical evolution of blockades at sea, in the air, and on land, for clarity's sake it is important to make a distinction between blockade operations as defined above and other types of economic warfare or coercion commonly considered similar to blockades. In defining what a blockade is, it is equally important to state what is *not* a blockade. Sanctions, embargoes, and sieges differ significantly from blockades, thus they are not included in the assessment of blockade operations.

Historical Blockades in Different Domains

This section examines the evolution of the concept of blockades at critical junctures through the centuries in order to understand how and why it has changed and to identify enduring elements for consideration in blockades in the future. It begins with naval blockades because that is where the international laws regarding blockades were first formed. Aerial blockades evolved using similar concepts, so they will be examined next, followed by land blockades and space blockades, which bear less resemblance to naval and aerial blockades. Finally, informational blockades will be examined in order to see how the theory of blockade has migrated outside of traditional, physical domains.

Naval Blockades

Naval blockades are the most relevant for cyberspace because at the height of maritime power, the maritime domain was the major avenue for the global transport of goods and information. States could not be world powers without significant maritime resources and the capability to defend their maritime dominance. Today, cyberspace is the major avenue for the global exchange of information (and by extension products), and any state that seeks to be a major player in the world system must have advanced cyber capabilities. The ability to deny entry into either of these domains is a key factor in maintaining global power and influence.

According to Maurice Parmelee, historian and member of the Blockade Committee during World War I, "[t]he purpose of a blockade is to isolate the enemy in such a fashion as to destroy its import and export trade. A blockaded nation is thus prevented from drawing supplies from other parts of the world and from sending to other countries its exportable surplus."[8] It is essentially a boycott. Furthermore, he says, "[a]n effective blockade excludes a nation temporarily from international trade, which means that it is deprived, for the time being, of the benefits of the world-wide system of division of labor which enables civilized nations to exchange their surplus products with one another."[9]

A naval blockade is an attempt to sever the nation's commercial and other economic relations with the remainder of the world, and it may be used as a method of isolating a nation.[10] The law and practice of blockade evolved with warfare since ancient times, but it has continuously represented the struggle of neutral states to safeguard their rights in times of war and belligerents who are prone to ignore neutral rights.

Blockades and the Rights of Neutrals

Codified blockade laws and operations evolved out of a desire to protect the rights of neutrals during conflict. The first proposed international rules of blockade date to 1780, when Russia presented them to the League of Armed Neutrality, whose goal was to protect neutral shipping against the British Royal Navy, which had a policy of unrestricted search of neutral shipping for French contraband during the American War of Independence.[11] During the Napoleonic Wars, England and France violated the rights of neutrals; around the same time, the United States became a seafaring country and began championing neutrals' rights. The issue of the rights of neutrals culminated in the Congress of Paris in 1856 and the Declaration of Paris Respecting Maritime Law, which abolished privateering, regulated relations between belligerents and neutrals, and introduced new rules for prize courts.[12]

The four basic rules of international law governing blockades were recognized by British Prize Courts before 1815:

- A blockade must be effective in order to be binding.
- Only a belligerent can establish a blockade.
- In order to be valid, a blockade must be declared and notified, its geographic limits stated, and a grace period provided to allow neutral vessels to exit.
- A blockade must be limited to the ports and coasts of the enemy.[13]

In addition, certain items were considered contraband or prohibited from trade. States could make their own contraband lists for each conflict, but with time, they grew quite complex. The Dutch jurist and philosopher Grotius organized commerce into three categories: goods that could only be used in war, goods not used in war and used only for pleasure, and goods that could be used both in and out of war (i.e., "dual-use" items, such as provisions, money, and ships). These categories helped to organize states' lists of contraband goods.[14]

There were two main issues associated with contraband to be debated: first, the nature of articles that could be confiscated; and second, the circumstances under which goods would be treated as a particular kind of good, whether in war or peace. These issues were and still are weighed against the belligerent's right to prevent foreign aid from reaching its enemy.[15]

International law and treaties emphasize the rights of belligerents and neutrals in blockade law because the critical issues of blockades centered on the rights of commerce in times of war. Throughout history, the blockade literature has sought to establish a balance between the rights of belligerent parties to make war on their enemies and the rights of neutral parties to continue with their businesses and remain outside of the conflict. Rules governing blockades were important for neutrals. Before the rules, neutrals could not refrain from trade with a belligerent nation for fear of being perceived as an ally of the enemy, but if they continued to trade with a belligerent, they risked danger and the perception that they were an ally of the belligerent. As a result, neutrals needed established laws or sets of practices to preserve their right to conduct commerce during times of conflict and protect them from the misperception of alliance with a belligerent.

The balance between the rights of belligerents and rights of neutrals has shifted over time. When the League of Armed Neutrality first broached the issue, the primary goal was to protect the rights of neutrals. As major powers rose and fell and technology changed the way blockades could be conducted, there was a movement toward the rights of belligerents, including the right of pursuit of blockade runners; the concept of "continuous voyage" was established during the Civil War, and long-distance blockades were constructed during World War II. As a result, the international laws of blockade are codified but not static; the history of blockade is one that reveals changing needs, priorities, technology, and adaptations of international legal and normative standards.

US Civil War

The United States' Civil War and the evolution of naval warfare to include steam-powered ships and heavy guns changed the rules of blockade. The Union began a blockade on the Confederacy on May 10, 1861; it involved 500 ships and 100,000 men, and over the course of four years, the Union captured ships and blockade runners valued at more than $30 million. However, the blockade never completely sealed off the South from the rest of the world, and the Confederacy imported enough war materials to sustain its armies.[16]

According to Civil War historian Craig L. Symonds, the Union blockade was different from most previous naval blockades. Historically, the purpose of many blockades was to keep the enemy's warships off the high seas and thereby secure safe passage for one's own commerce. Yet the Confederate Navy was too small to try to contain, and the Union realized it could have more of an impact preventing trade than keeping warships in port.[17] The purpose of the Union's blockade was to seal off the enemy's coast to trade and, according to Lincoln, "prevent entrance and exit of vessels" for all ports in the south. Ironically, the declaration of a blockade was tantamount to a de facto recognition of a Confederate government (which Lincoln protested vigorously) because the international maritime law stated that blockades must be between belligerent states.

Blockade running became a thriving business during the Civil War, and in order to catch and deter blockade runners, the Union Navy needed to adopt new strategies of blockades, both along its coast and on the high seas.[18] The *Springbok* case firmly established the doctrine of continuous voyage as a principle of blockades.[19] This case established that goods with the ultimate destination of enemy ports are liable to confiscation at any point along the journey—even at neutral points en route to enemy ports—not just in enemy territorial waters. This made interdiction on the high seas more important than ever and proved advantageous years later when the British were successful in stopping the greater part of Germany's overseas trade.[20]

In the end, the blockade was the Union's greatest commitment to the naval war, as it absorbed huge resources and required an expansion of the navy. The blockade contributed to the economic and psychological isolation and depression of the Confederacy, yet it was not decisive in the outcome of the war, according to some historians, who characterize it as a form of slow asphyxiation that was successful only when combined with other measures of warfare.[21]

Early Twentieth Century

The Russo-Japanese War of 1904–05 introduced practices that disregarded neutrals' rights and blatantly endangered their lives. These practices included the exclusion of neutrals from certain areas of the high seas, the sinking of neutral prizes, indiscriminate undersea mining of strategic areas, and extended contraband lists.[22] Previously, blockades were a form of total warfare against the enemy's military and civilian population; with the Russo-Japanese War, neutral ships and countries also felt the immediate effects of the blockade.

In 1914, neutral ships were permitted by international law to continue to trade freely with belligerents, but they had to submit to the right of search and could be brought before a prize court if they offered resistance to search, carried contraband, rendered aid to the enemy, or attempted to infringe on a blockade.[23] Goods were only considered contraband if they were of a specific (predetermined) nature. The *Kim* case of 1915 established that goods could be considered contraband because their final destination was an enemy government or armed forces. Thus, the destination of the items alone could determine whether they were contraband and susceptible to confiscation by a belligerent.[24]

World War I

During World War I, the blockade had a diplomatic, economic, and financial character. It was designed to apply pressure to Germany by limiting the tonnage of certain goods delivered to the country. Maritime trade was important to Germany's economy and power. When war was declared, the vast majority of its trade (including cargo of imports and exports) was outside of Germany, not stockpiled at home, thus creating an immediate trade imbalance and a strategic risk for Germany.[25]

To conform to international law, a blockade must be effective and bear with equal severity upon all neutrals. This requirement proved difficult with the British blockade of Germany during World War I because it proved difficult to impose a blockade on the long coastline of the Baltic states. In the strictest legal sense, the Central Empires were never blockaded during World War I; instead, it was economic encirclement.[26]

The declaration of submarine warfare dramatically changed World War I and the imposition of the blockade. The British imposed a blockade on Germany at the beginning of the war. In 1915, Germany began using submarine warfare tactics against the British blockade, targeting any hostile merchant ships in British or Irish waters, including the English Channel, and destroying them without regard for crew or passengers.[27]

Submarine warfare effectively reversed the blockade by endangering cargo headed to Britain, thus placing Britain in a position of being unable to receive all of its shipments. In January 1917, Germany declared a policy of unrestricted submarine warfare, which expanded the war to other waters and states. Less than a month after this declaration of unrestricted warfare, President Wilson broke diplomatic relations with Germany. In April 1917, the United States declared war on Germany after three American steamers had been torpedoed by German submarines in the previous three months.[28]

It is impossible to determine with accuracy the extent to which the blockade was responsible for victory in the war, but according to historians, it was effective in diminishing the number of goods that made it to the Central Empires. After the United States declared war on Germany, the blockade became simple: it forbade any exportation whatsoever to neutral countries adjacent to Germany. Allies proceeded to exchange products with the same neutrals only if the latter were able to supply them with goods that were useful to them and their war effort.[29]

The enemy's preparedness for the blockade made a significant difference in its ability to withstand it because stockpiles would allow both the military and civilian population to survive. According to some historians, the German perspective is that the defeat of Germany in World War I was due—almost without exception—to the blockade. Counterfactually, if Germany's counterblockade of Great Britain (unrestricted submarine warfare) had been successful and allied and neutral ships had been sunk at a rapid rate, Britain would have been isolated and paralyzed and cut off from the flow of supplies from the United States, and Germany may have won the war.[30]

While it is impossible to know if this would have truly been the case, it is an indication of the importance of blockades and the geographical location of a country. In Sir Eyre Crowe's Memorandum on the Present State of British Relations with France and Germany in 1907, he wrote, "The general character of England's foreign policy is determined by the immutable conditions of her geographical situation on the ocean flank of Europe as an island State with vast oversea colonies and dependencies, whose existence and survival as an independent community are inseparably bound up with the possession of preponderant sea power."[31] Winston Churchill, as first lord of the admiralty, invested the nation's resources in building a strong, modern fleet.

Blockades are a type of total warfare, whereby the entire population of Germany suffered because of the blockades due to German policy choices, and the realities of modern warfare. The effects of blockade were to starve the German people and disable their industries. German economic life collapsed by the end of 1916, but the German army was still well equipped.[32] According to historian Lieutenant Louis Guichard, "[e]conomic encirclement after all was only an achievement incidental to the successful accomplishment by the Allied navies of their main task of acquiring and maintaining the mastery of the seas, without which victory would have been impossible."[33] Thus, encirclement and blockade were one part of the war effort that resulted in mastery of a particular domain that was essential to victory.

World War II

A similar type of economic warfare played a major part of World War II, proving that the success of an economic blockade depends on three factors. First, the economy of the blockaded power must be vulnerable. Second, the blockading power must have the means, by control of sea and land routes, diplomatic influence, control at source, or other ways, to cut off the supply of goods to its enemy from outside its border. Third, the blockading power must be able to secure the acquiescence or cooperation of neutral powers, whether adjacent to the enemy or supplying it from overseas.[34]

World War II was important to the development of economic warfare and blockades because Germany effectively controlled the entire continent of Europe. The basic assumption of the Allies was that Germany could be bled to death slowly via economic warfare.[35] Britain's Ministry of Economic Warfare defined economic warfare as a military operation with the objective of defeating the enemy by depriving it of the material means of resistance. It uses direct attacks as well as indirect pressure on neutral countries from which it draws supplies, which makes it distinct from coercive measures used in times of peace.[36]

Economic warfare could be conducted through legislative action (i.e., domestic policy changes), diplomatic action (i.e., persuading neutrals not to trade with the enemy), and military action. Military action could involve blockades, capture of ships or cargoes, contraband control, direct attacks on ports, invasion of important economic areas, attacks on shipping on the high seas, and attacks on centers of storage, production, manufacturing, or distribution. All three approaches interfered with the enemy's acquisition of goods from overseas.[37]

Post–World War II

Blockades continued to be used after World War II, albeit in new and different circumstances. In 1950, President Truman ordered a close naval blockade of North Korea within a week after the invasion to cut off seaborne maneuvers and close its seaborne supply lines. This blockade was a UN naval blockade under a UN charter, which means that it did not qualify as an act of war. But a unilateral US blockade would have been an act of war and could have provoked a Soviet response.[38]

In 1958, the UN Conference on the Law of the Sea produced the Geneva Conventions on the High Seas. It comprised a statement of the rules of conduct to which all nations should subscribe and included a statement that a blockade could not be instituted unless war had already begun between the parties.[39]

CUBAN MISSILE CRISIS

The Cuban Missile Crisis of 1962 resulted in a selective naval blockade that prohibited the shipment of offensive weapons to Cuba but did not prohibit food, petroleum, or other goods. The weakness of the blockade was that it could not remove the missiles; for that, diplomatic measures and military threats were employed. This operation was not targeted at economic or commercial trade but was successful at applying significant pressure through seapower.[40]

During the crisis, the term *blockade* was eschewed in favor of *quarantine* (or *defensive quarantine*) for several reasons. The legal implications of a blockade at the time were that blockades were only recognized as legitimate after a formal declaration of war by the blockading power—and the United States was seeking to avoid war with the Soviet Union. Second, the quarantine of Cuba was partial and applied only to specific offensive military equipment, unlike previous blockades. Finally, there was consensus that the term *quarantine* sounded less bellicose than *blockade* and was therefore more acceptable to Latin American partners and the international community.[41] The distinctions between *quarantine* and *blockade* highlight key features of the understanding of blockade at that time.

UN NAVAL BLOCKADE OPERATIONS: VIETNAM, IRAQ, AND LIBYA

In 1965, the United States authorized the navy to search and seize enemy supply vessels along the coast of South Vietnam. Before 1972, it was politically unacceptable to stop vessels in North Vietnam, so the navy had to do it in the South. Operation "Market Time" was a three-tiered barrier operation that included air patrol, off-shore combat ships, and inshore patrols. Interdiction rates at sea were high, but the effectiveness of the operation was difficult to determine because the Viet Cong developed alternate lines of communication and supply and increased shipments overland and via the river system.[42]

In 1972, President Nixon announced that the United States would begin to blockade North Vietnam. Operation Pocket Money closed three major ports in North Vietnam for 300 days, halted all exports from North Vietnam, and decreased imports by 30 percent. Its goal was to interdict supplies to the North Vietnamese Army as it prepared for the invasion of South Vietnam known as the Easter Offensive (or Nguyen Hue Offensive). This blockade was achieved by mining the ports, which allowed naval vessels to operate elsewhere. Although the mining of the ports had been controversial within the Nixon administration, and the operation was denounced by the Soviet Union and China, it was a success in the end. The blockade was deemed operationally effective and assisted with the overall war effort by forcing North Vietnam to rely more on roads and railways to transport goods, which, in turn, improved the effectiveness of the US air bombing campaign in North Vietnam.[43] In addition to affecting military operations, Operation Pocket Money had serious effects on the North Vietnamese economy and provided Nixon with a powerful negotiating lever at the Paris Peace Talks.[44]

During the 1990–91 Gulf War, the UN established a naval blockade against Iraq (and Kuwait during the occupation). On August 26, 1990, the UN adopted Security Council Resolution 665 to impose sanctions on Iraq and halt shipping to and from the country. Specifically, it called upon member states and their deployed maritime forces to "halt all inward and outward maritime shipping" and inspect it for compliance with earlier resolutions that placed an embargo on trade with Iraq for all goods except those with medical or humanitarian purposes.[45] No trade would enter or leave Iraq by sea, and all ships would be inspected by coalition forces, which had authority to use military force to prevent blockade running.[46] Ships and airplanes from fourteen states intercepted and challenged more than 7,500 merchant ships. After the war, the United States and other nations continued to blockade Iraq in order to enforce UN sanctions against the regime of Saddam Hussein.[47]

In 2011, the UN again approved a naval blockade, this time against Libya and the regime of Muammar Gadhafi. In the face of popular protests against the regime, Gadhafi answered the unrest with the use of overwhelming force against civilians and rebels. The UN responded with Security Council Resolution 1973, which called for the enforcement of an arms embargo against Libya by all member states. The enforcement authorized the use of all necessary force against vessels suspected of carrying restricted goods to or from Libya and led to the construction of a blockade. In this particular case, the blockade and embargo specifically targeted arms and related material.[48] The goal of the blockade was to limit Gadhafi's supply of weapons and prevent the reinforcements necessary to continue the fight against the rebels.[49]

Israeli Blockade of the Gaza Strip

When Hamas was elected to power in June 2007, Israel imposed a blockade on the Gaza Strip as retribution for Hamas's antagonistic policies toward Israel, which included firing rockets into Israeli territory. The goal of the blockade was to force regime change in Gaza through collective punishment of its people. Approximately 80 percent of the 1.5 million people who live in Gaza depend upon food aid, including the 45 percent of the population who are younger than age 15. The ban on exports and most imports quickly destroyed 98 percent of Gaza's industry and has since hampered recovery and reconstruction.[50]

As a consequence of the blockade, Israel was permitted to stop ships on the high seas that it believed were destined for Gaza. A UN panel found this to be a lawful exercise of self-defense in the context of an armed conflict. According to the report, "[t]he fundamental principle of the freedom of navigation on the high seas is subject to only certain limited exceptions under international law. Israel faces a threat to its security from militant groups in Gaza. The naval blockade was imposed as a legitimate security measure in order to prevent weapons from entering Gaza by sea and its implementation complied with the requirements of international law."[51] However, the panel's conclusions were not definitive in fact or law because it did not have the ability to compel testimony or demand documents.[52]

Israel eased the restrictions of the blockade in 2010 in response to international pressure following several attempts of nongovernmental organization (NGO) flotillas to break the blockade. The relaxed conditions of the blockade allow nonmilitary and dual-use items to be imported to Gaza, but there is still a restriction on construction materials. An investigation by the United Nations Office for the Coordination of Humanitarian affairs found that the new restrictions did not allow for substantial improvement in people's lives.[53]

The Israeli blockade of Gaza presents an interesting case of what could be considered a "defensive blockade." Blockades are traditionally against belligerent nations (even pacific blockades) for the purpose of applying economic and military pressure. The blockade of the Gaza Strip was not against a state, yet it is internationally recognized as a legal blockade.

Aerial Blockades

The concept of aerial blockades has been discussed since the early years of military airpower.[54] Aerial blockades represent a significant evolution in the practice of blockades. In the past, evolution in naval blockades reflected new naval technology (ships powered by steam or coal, for instance, were able to interdict other vessels on the high seas). With the advent of air power, blockades were adapted to fit not just new technology, but also a new domain.[55] An examination of the evolution of aerial blockades is useful to understand how technological innovation opened a new domain for human interaction and changed the practice of blockades to accommodate the specific attributes of that domain—a process similar to the one that currently exists in cyberspace with respect to cyber blockades.

During World War II, airpower became an important source of military power. According to Italian general Giulio Douhet, "aeronautics opened up to men a new field of action, the field of the air. In so doing it of necessity created a new battlefield; for wherever two men meet, conflict is inevitable."[56] Alexander P. De Seversky described the emergence of aviation as "the paramount and decisive factor" in war.[57] These early theorists of airpower focused on the new principles of warfare that were influenced by the emergence of military aviation. As Douhet reminded readers and military planners, "the form of any war . . . depends upon the technical means of war available."[58]

In his seminal work, De Seversky described the importance of aerial blockades, an argument that was influenced by observation of the German blockade against Britain and its use of airpower in extending the range of the blockade. De Seversky asserted quite clearly that "the blockade of an enemy nation has become a function of air power" and is "destined to be the only effective type of blockade."[59] He described three distinct advantages of aerial blockades. First, aircraft can harass shipping at both ends of the sea routes—at the ports of origin and destination—whereas naval blockades generally focus solely on the targeted territory. Second, their speed allows them to act quickly, and they are able to harass more ships in a given time period. Third, because of their speed, aircraft can engage in joint operations with naval forces as the directing or commanding component, thus increasing overall operational effectiveness.[60]

In surveying the damage done to the British war effort (to include merchant and military vessels), De Seversky estimated that approximately 25 to 30 percent of the destruction rendered by the blockade of Britain during a two-year period was attributable to airpower. Throughout that period, the proportion of destruction rendered by airpower continually expanded. He reasoned that the only successful countermeasure for aerial blockade is greater aviation power because opposing airpower can diminish the opponent's ability to conduct an aerial blockade.[61]

While naval blockades prevent commerce by preventing ingress and egress of ports and harbors, aerial blockade can be effective at any spot in the ocean, providing that the aircraft has sufficient striking range. Furthermore, naval blockades maintain an external barrier to lines of communication, but an "aerial blockade is immeasurably more effective in that it affects both outside and interior breach of supply lines simultaneously. It is total and instantaneous blockade." Thus, internal and external supply lines and lines of communication could be affected through the use of airpower.[62]

In reality, air blockades have not been as common as naval or land blockades and have been used somewhat differently. Like naval and land blockades, air blockades involve denial of the airspace in order to prevent egress and ingress. Also, they are frequently used in conjunction with naval blockades and other forms of economic pressure, such as embargos or sanctions.

In the post–World War II era, aerial blockade operations have been limited mostly to military operations other than war (with the exception of the Lebanon case, as will be shown below). Several of these operations have been humanitarian interventions designed to provide assistance to civilians or to forces engaged in armed combat within a state. These operations are commonly referred to as "no-fly zones" (NFZs) because they establish an area of exclusion in the air.[63] In all cases, the primary task was to establish air dominance in order to implement an aerial exclusion zone as a form of area denial or anti-access operation.

Iraq: Operation Southern Watch (1992–2003) and Operation Northern Watch (1997–2003)

Operation Southern Watch began on August 27, 1992, and was conducted by the Joint Task Force for Southwest Asia to enforce an NFZ south of the thirty-second parallel.[64] The mission of the operation was to prevent Iraqi forces from using airpower against Iraqi civilians, specifically to end the bombing and strafing of Shia Muslims in southern Iraq by the Iraqi Air Force after the 1990–91 Gulf War.

The NFZ was deemed necessary because a disproportionate force was used against the civilian population in violation of international norms and laws. The NFZ could be considered a pacific aerial blockade intended to coerce Iraq into a new course of action. The stated purpose of the NFZ was outlined in United Nations Security Council Resolution (UNSCR) 688, passed in April 1991, which condemned the repression of the civilian population and demanded that Iraq immediately end the repression. It also authorized the UN secretary-general to pursue humanitarian efforts in Iraq and use all resources at his disposal to address the needs of the Iraqi population.[65] This resolution was viewed as the political authorization to establish an NFZ in Iraq; it was named Operation Southern Watch, in which the United States, the United Kingdom, France, and Saudi Arabia participated.[66]

UNSCR 688 also led to Operation Provide Comfort, which was designed to protect Kurds fleeing their homes in northern Iraq and to provide humanitarian aid to them in the aftermath of the Gulf War. Operation Provide Comfort was followed in 1997 by Operation Northern Watch, a US and European combined task force responsible for enforcing an NFZ over the airspace of Iraq north of the thirty-sixth parallel and preventing Iraqi aggression toward Kurds.[67]

The United States, the United Kingdom, and Turkey participated in Operation Northern Watch. For the first two years, relatively little combat was required to enforce the NFZ. After Operation Desert Fox in December 1998, Iraqi forces began firing on coalition aircraft, and low-level conflict ensued until 2003. The operation officially concluded on May 1, 2003, after US and coalition forces invaded Iraq and overthrew the government of Saddam Hussein.

These NFZs were the first to be implemented in the post–Cold War era and the first to receive international support. A key feature of the NFZ is that they were implemented to reduce state capacity and deter or prevent military abuse of power against civilian populations. The aerial blockades were implemented in conjunction with economic sanctions and naval interdiction; collectively, they were able to target military and commercial activities, so as to weaken the state militarily and economically, while providing assistance to the civilian population.

Bosnia: Operation Deny Flight (1993–95)

NATO conducted Operation Deny Flight from April 12, 1993, through December 20, 1995. This operation prevented warring parties from using "belligerent air" as a medium of warfare in order to protect the civilian population. The mission began as enforcement of an NFZ over Bosnia and Herzegovina to prevent the use of airpower during the conflict, but it evolved to include close air support for UN troops in Bosnia. [68]

UNSCR 618 authorized the use of "all necessary measures" to enforce the NFZ. The mission of the operation was threefold: First, it banned flights by "all fixed-wing and rotary-wing aircraft in the airspace of Bosnia-Herzegovina," meaning that all aircraft were prohibited from ingress and egress from Bosnian airspace unless specifically approved by the UN Flight Coordination Center in Zaghreb. Second, it was "to provide close air support to UN troops on the ground at the request of, and controlled by, United Nations forces." Third, the mission aimed "to conduct . . . air strikes against designated targets threatening the security of the UN-declared safe areas."[69]

The operation began with aircraft from France, the Netherlands, and the United States. Throughout the 983 days of the operation, Belgium, Canada, Denmark, France, Germany, Italy, the Netherlands, Norway, Spain, Turkey, the United Kingdom, and the United States deployed forces in support of

Operation Deny Flight. NATO aircraft were based in France, Germany, Greece, Italy, and the United Kingdom and on carriers in the Adriatic Sea. A total of 4,500 personnel from twelve NATO countries participated in the operation.[70]

Operation Deny Flight was significant for this study of cyber blockades for several reasons. It was an aerial blockade and the first military combat engagement in NATO's history, which helped establish a relationship between the UN and NATO. In addition, it established air dominance over Bosnia, which enabled Operation Deliberate Force, the NATO bombing campaign in Bosnia that played a key role in ending the war. Militarily, the operation was successful, preventing fixed-wing aircraft from flying over Bosnia and Herzegovina; however, there were hundreds of violations by helicopters that would land when warned by NATO fighters, only to resume flight after NATO forces departed the area.[71] Politically, the operation was successful because it led to the political resolution of the war. According to Michael Beale, "the operation's implied objective was to demonstrate UN and NATO determination to stabilize the situation in Bosnia so that a peaceful settlement could be achieved."[72]

Lebanon War (2006)

During the 2006 war between Israel and Lebanon, Israel imposed naval and aerial blockades on Lebanon. The goal of the blockades was to prevent the freedom of navigation in and out of Lebanese ports and airspace, with the exception of humanitarian supply ships and vessels to evacuate refugees from Lebanon.[73] The aerial blockade restricted normal air traffic from entering Lebanon in an attempt to prevent arms shipments from reaching Hezbollah forces in Lebanon. Many criticized the blockade for hampering the delivery of humanitarian relief supplies and imports required to rebuild the civilian infrastructure damaged during the war.[74] The blockades lasted nearly two months, from July 13 to September 7, 2006.[75]

Unlike the NFZs of Iraq and Bosnia, the aerial blockade in Lebanon was unilateral and not aimed at protecting civilians. It was intended primarily to prevent the transfer of military equipment and supplies to Hezbollah forces in Lebanon, although nonmilitary trade was also caught in the blockade. This type of aerial blockade more closely resembles naval blockades between belligerents in the nineteenth century than the NFZs that preceded it, but both are considered types of aerial blockades.

Libyan Uprising (2011)

In 2011, an uprising against Gadhafi's regime began in eastern Libya. In the midst of the "Arab Spring" that led to massive unrest throughout the region and the resignations of Ben Ali in Tunisia and Musharraf in Egypt, Gadhafi attempted to crush the uprising with military force. The rebels in eastern Libya fought back, but they were confronted with massive military force, including airpower, used by the Gadhafi regime.

A few weeks after the uprising began, the United Nations Security Council, with the support of the Arab League, voted to implement an NFZ over Libya. The NFZ banned all flights in the airspace of Libya, except for humanitarian relief flights, including the delivery of food and the evacuation of refugees. UNSCR 1970/1973 gave member states the authority to use "all necessary means" to enforce the NFZ and protect civilians. Furthermore, the resolution established an arms embargo against Libya, preventing the transportation of arms to or from the Libyan Army.[76]

The NATO aircraft enforcing the NFZ actively prevented Libyan military aircraft from operating in the airspace and other aircraft from delivering supplies to the Libyan military or government. As a self-defense measure, NATO forces destroyed air defense systems throughout Libya and any ground forces that posed a threat to aircraft. In addition, they destroyed Gadhafi's forces and equipment that threatened civilians and allowed for the safe delivery of humanitarian aid to the Libyan population.[77]

As a tactical measure, the NFZ gave the rebels a window of reprieve in which they could regroup and reorganize their efforts in order to redress the balance of power. Airpower was critical to the Libyan military's ability to project power throughout the country, and the military's unopposed aerial bombardment of rebels and civilians was a significant and decisive asymmetrical advantage for the Gadhafi regime. As a result, the NFZ seriously impeded the Libyan military's capabilities.[78]

The NFZ and its accompanying naval blockade lasted from March 31 until October 31, 2011. The United States, France, Greece, Italy, Norway, the United Kingdom, and Qatar were some of the countries that deployed forces in support of the NATO operation.[79] NATO Secretary General Anders Fogh Rasmussen said of the mission, "We have fully complied with the historic mandate of the United Nations to protect the people of Libya, to enforce the no-fly zone and the arms embargo . . . . Operation Unified Protector is one of the most successful in NATO history."[80]

Land Blockades

The international law literature generally limits blockades to the maritime and aerial domains, but history has given us many examples of blockades on land. As a result, scholars debate whether true blockades, in the sense of naval and air blockades, have been or can be implemented on land. This debate is useful because it highlights the different aspects and attributes of the land domain and the specific challenges that accompany blockades on land. The differences between land and other domains may also be present in cyberspace and challenge us to expand our understanding of blockades.

Many scholars use the word *blockade* to describe events on land that are similar to naval blockades, whereas others argue that these "blockades" are actually sieges or other types of land warfare and thus do not constitute blockades. In addition, a review of the United States Department of Defense *Joint Publication 1-02*, last updated in August 2011, reveals that the word *blockade* is not used or defined anywhere in that document. The *Joint Publication 1-02* is considered the definitional authority on all modern military operations. The word with the closest meaning to *blockade* was *interception*, and those definitions were limited to air, maritime, and electronic interceptions.[81]

This ambiguity may have something to do with blockades on land not being frequently used in warfare, especially modern warfare. Modern armies are tactical maneuver teams, and their tactics, techniques, and procedures have changed significantly since the end of World War II to no longer include blockades. Even before the end of World War II, land blockades were not a common military operation. In the literature they are often linked to sieges and types of total warfare that were more common centuries ago, while there are few examples of stand-alone blockades on land.

In ancient warfare, invading armies established blockades to prevent a city or region from receiving reinforcements and additional supplies and then laid siege to the city, rendering the near-total destruction of the people and property within. These "blockades" were conducted as part of a larger operation with the ultimate goal of destroying people and property (a goal that is now illegal under international law).[82] In this context, land blockades were part of a campaign of total warfare that indiscriminately killed civilians and military personnel alike.[83]

According to historian Paul Kern, ancient siege warfare was total war, pitting entire societies against one another, blurring the distinction between battlefield and society, engulfing women and children in the violence, destroying society's infrastructure, and uprooting entire populations.[84] Interestingly, he sees this ancient type of warfare as foreshadowing modern warfare because violence is not limited to soldiers on the battlefield.

Other scholars have associated land blockades with the forced movement of people: blockades are intended to cause suffering within the civilian population and to force them to leave a territory. Hugo Slim suggests that "the two main ways of using food and starvation as weapons of war are through policies of blockade or scorched earth—the former often being a more subtle and more easily disguised form of the latter . . . blockade was epitomized by siege warfare in earlier days by the deliberate control of key market routes or the cornering and stockpiling of core commodities like grain and rice."[85]

In order to conduct an investigation of historical blockades in different domains, this section will examine two major military operations that are commonly referred to as land blockades: the Blockade of Leningrad and the Berlin Blockade. The purpose of this examination is to understand what happened in both cases in order to analyze the events and identify how they are similar to and different from other types of blockades.

Blockade of Leningrad

The lengthy, entrenched blockade of Leningrad was unusual during World War II, which was a war characterized by the mobility of forces during military operations. Besieging cities and starving populations had ceased to be a major form of warfare over a century earlier, when sieges were rendered less effective by the massive defensive walls that protected the inhabitants. In the twentieth century, the sieges that did occur, such as the Leningrad siege, focused on cities that were military strong points and often strategic seaports, which were also advantageous to the enemy.[86]

The blockade of Leningrad, also known as the siege of Leningrad, began on September 8, 1941, and lasted for 872 days. It was one of the longest and most destructive sieges in history and one of the deadliest in terms of casualties. The blockade disrupted utility, water, energy, and food supplies and resulted in the deaths of over 1 million people.[87] Approximately 650,000 Leningraders died from hunger, cold, and illness in the first year of the blockade alone.[88]

The Nazi German forces wanted to capture Leningrad (now St. Petersburg) because of its strategic importance as the main base of the Soviet Baltic fleet, its industrial strength and arms factories, and its political significance as the former capital of Russia and the symbolic capital of the Russian Revolution. It was the second-largest city in Russia and a major industrial and cultural center. Hitler was keen on the destruction of the cities of Leningrad and Stalingrad in particular because he believed they were the "breeding places of Bolshevism."[89]

With the help of Finnish military forces who blocked the northern route from Leningrad, German forces were able to achieve a near-total encirclement of the city.[90] The only outlet was a winter ice road over Lake Ladoga, which was constantly under threat of German bombs. By mid-September 1941, German troops had cut off all road and rail access to the city and trapped its 3.2 to 3.8 million inhabitants inside.[91]

The purpose of the siege was to destroy the city of Leningrad in order to weaken Russian power. During the siege, civilians tried to flee the city, but the German forces turned them back. A letter from the German naval chief of staff reported that Hitler had decided that "the problem of the life of the population and the provisioning of them is a problem which cannot and must not be decided by us . . . . We are not interested in preserving even a part of the population of this large city."[92] Hitler is quoted as saying, "We have no interest in saving lives of the civilian population" and "Leningrad must die of starvation."[93] As the Nazi directive on "The Future of the City of Petersburg" stated, "The Fuehrer has decided to wipe the city of Petersburg from the face of the earth." It describes a blockade to secure the city, after which it would be subjected to artillery bombardment and constant bombing so as to raze it to the ground. It also decreed that if the city requested capitulation, the request would be denied by the Germans.[94] At the same time, there is little evidence that Stalin ever seriously entertained the option of surrendering Leningrad in order to spare it damage or destruction.[95]

Over 1 million people died in the siege, and 1.4 million (mostly women and children) were evacuated via the dangerous ice road over Lake Ladoga, many of whom died as a result of starvation or bombardment along the road. Civilians in the city suffered from extreme starvation; in January and February 1942, as many as 700 to 1,000 people died every day, mostly of starvation. Reports of cannibalism appeared that same winter, and the Leningrad police created a special unit to combat cannibalism. Estimates of the economic destruction and human loss of life in the Siege of Leningrad exceeded those of the Battle of Stalingrad, Battle of Moscow, and atomic bombs of Hiroshima and Nagasaki. Some historians view it as genocide through "a racially motivated starvation policy" against the people of the Soviet Union.[96]

The counteroffensive of Soviet troops outside of Leningrad began in 1942, and the encirclement was broken in January 1943. The Soviet forces were able to establish a 10- to 12-kilometer-wide land corridor to provide relief to the people of Leningrad. The siege itself did not end until January 27, 1944, when the Soviet Army expelled German forces from their position south of the city.[97] After the war, a tribunal acquitted the German commander Feldmarschall Wilhelm Ritter von Leeb of war crimes on the grounds that it was lawful (but extreme) to drive fleeing noncombatants back into a besieged place if the besieged commander expelled the civilians in order to conserve supplies to prolong the fight.[98]

Berlin Blockade

The Berlin Blockade of 1948–49 was the result of a gap in international law and treaty agreements governing the use of land and water access to Berlin. The Soviets used this gap to their strategic advantage to cut off Berlin. The Berlin Airlift was intended to be a short-term measure until a negotiated settlement could be reached, but it proved so successful as a counterblockade that the Soviets ultimately realized the blockade was ineffective and becoming a liability.[99]

The Berlin Blockade, which lasted from June 24, 1948, to May 12, 1949, was the first major international crisis of the post–World War II era. According to the Potsdam Agreement, Berlin was divided into four sectors, each to be temporarily controlled by one of the Allies: France, the Soviet Union, Great Britain, and the United States. As it happened, the Soviet sector produced much of the food supplies for the rest of Berlin.[100]

In the confusion and haste at the end of the war, allied planners overlooked the creation of a formal, written agreement negotiating overland access to Berlin, which was located 100 miles inside the larger Soviet zone of occupation. Several factors contributed to this omission: the general assumption that the occupation would not last long; the importance of other issues; Soviet recognition of the right of Western access to Berlin since the occupation began; and misplaced trust in Soviet goodwill. For eight weeks following the surrender of Berlin, the Soviets denied Western access to the city while they subjected Berliners to brutal treatment at the hands of the Soviet Army. After two months, the Soviets granted Western forces permission to use one railway, one road, and one air corridor to access Berlin. Within a few months, this was further restricted to just one railway with a limited number of trains per day.[101] These restrictions created immediate tension among the former allies.

In 1947, the United States created the European Recovery Act, or "Marshall Plan," to provide comprehensive assistance to any European nation that wanted to participate. Stalin viewed the Marshall Plan as a plan for American economic penetration and increased political and cultural influence, so he refused to allow the Soviet Union or its satellite states to participate. By early 1948, the Western powers determined that Soviet influence in eastern Germany was so widespread that West Berlin was in danger of falling to Soviet influence in the future. In order to prevent this, they deemed it necessary to integrate West Germany's economy with that of Western Europe, which had adopted the Marshall Plan.[102]

In order to do this, the Western powers began making plans for a new currency in the West Berlin sectors. The currency that was established at the end of the war had been so significantly devalued by excessive Soviet printing that a new currency was to play a crucial role by stabilizing West Germany's economy and allowing it to integrate with the economy of Western Europe. In response to these plans, the Russian government began planning for the introduction of new currency into the Soviet zone.[103] On June 22, 1948, in the midst of the currency crisis, the Soviet delegate told the other occupying powers, "We are warning both you and the population of Berlin that we shall apply economic and administrative sanctions that will lead to the circulation in Berlin exclusively of the currency of the Soviet occupation zone."[104]

Two days later, on June 24, 1948, the Soviets severed land and water communications between the Soviet zone and the Western zones and stopped all rail and barge traffic to and from Berlin. The following day, the Soviets stopped supplying food to the other sectors of Berlin. Surface traffic to Berlin from the Western sectors was prevented, electricity was cut off, and only air corridors remained open. At the time the blockade was established, West Berlin had thirty-six days' worth of food and enough coal to last forty-five days.[105]

The purpose of the blockade, according to US Air Force historian Roger Miller, was to reverse the political decision regarding currency, not to force Western powers out of Berlin, although that was a long-term goal of the Soviet government. Based on his actions and options (including that the United States had the atomic bomb and Moscow did not), it was clear that

Stalin wanted to avoid a war with the United States and other Western powers but was willing to use every method short of war in order to achieve his political objectives. Likewise, the United States sought to avoid a war with the Soviet Union. Therefore, after considering its response to the blockade of Berlin, it eschewed armed convoys and forced entry into the city in favor of a (seemingly temporary) solution that would not escalate the situation but would fully utilize the rights and access that were negotiated and guaranteed in formal agreements with the Soviet Union.[106]

The American and British response to the Berlin Blockade was an airlift to provide short-term relief to the Western powers' garrisons located within Berlin, as well as support the population of Berlin as best they could, until a political agreement could be reached. The Berlin Airlift, as it became known, was intended to be a stopgap measure that would give Western powers time to negotiate a new agreement with the Soviet Union.[107]

The airlift was aided by the loose application of the land blockade of Berlin. West Berlin was not completely isolated from the Soviet sector: the train wound its way in and out of both sides, rivers passed through multiple sectors, and thousands of Berliners crossed sectors every day to go to work. A thriving black market for Western goods developed in the Soviet sector, and West Berliners were able to buy goods from that sector. Soviet forces made attempts to reroute trains and search people, but faced with the sheer number of people—80,000—who crossed from one side to the other each day, it was impossible to fully implement or regulate the blockade within the city of Berlin.[108]

The sectors were economically interdependent, a fact that the Western powers used to their advantage in establishing a counterblockade in West Berlin. When the Soviet sector halted milk delivery to the Western sectors, the Western powers ceased meat delivery to the Soviet sector—and milk delivery quickly resumed. When the Soviets announced that food would not be delivered outside of the Soviet sector, the Western powers halted delivery of food and medicine to the Soviet sector. Because West Berlin received sufficient quantities of food and fuel from the airlift, the tit-for-tat negotiations had little impact there; however, the counterblockade had significant impact on the economy of the Soviet sector, which was not receiving external food supplies.[109] Thus, there was a blockade and a counterblockade, but neither was completely enforced because the city's sectors were so interdependent.

The blockade continued until May 12, 1949. The Western powers began the Berlin Airlift in June 1948 as a small operation of 80 tons of cargo, but by the following April, crews were working around the clock to deliver 8,893 tons of supplies per day—more than had previously arrived by rail and plenty of supplies for the people of West Berlin.[110] In the end, the Berlin Airlift delivered more than 2.3 million tons of cargo to Berlin and carried almost 82 thousand tons of cargo out of Berlin on more than 277 thousand flights.[111] The airlift was such as success that it rendered the land blockade ineffective and became a disaster for the policies of Joseph Stalin and a source of embarrassment for the Soviet Union.[112]

Modern "Blockade" Operations

According to *Joint Publication 1-02*, modern armies do not lay siege to entire cities or regions or conduct blockades.[113] Instead, they use checkpoints to monitor the flow of goods and people in and out of a region and employ tactical forces to strike at enemy targets hidden among civilian populations. In recent operations, the US Army conducted interdiction operations to find drug smugglers in northern Afghanistan, capture Taliban and al-Qaeda fighters in Afghanistan, and monitor the goods entering and exiting cities in Iraq and Afghanistan.[114]

The interdiction operations of the US military in Afghanistan and Iraq have been for the purposes of law enforcement, security, stability, and reconstruction. Most of the contraband goods or people they seek to interdict include illicit drugs, weapons, and known criminals or terrorists. As a result, interdiction operations cannot be considered blockades because they do not focus on preventing the state from legitimately exchanging goods and products with other states or from growing its economy; rather, they focus on interdicting actors who operate outside of the rule of law and smuggle goods and people across borders.

Space Blockade

Another domain important to examine is space. Unlike the previous three domains, space is important not because of a rich history of blockades in space (in fact, there is not one), but rather because of the nexus of technology and geography. In other domains, the role of technology in exploration and exploitation may be taken for granted because it has been around for so long (e.g., no one alive today remembers when the first sailing ship was invented), but space has opened to human beings much more recently because of the advances in modern technology. Technology altered the specific relationship between humans and space—just as it has altered, indeed created, the relationship between humans and cyberspace. Discussions of space remind that the geography and physical attributes of the environment, such as gravity, remain important to understanding different aspects and limitations of the domain, as well as power relationships among the states that seek to exploit it.[115]

The discussion of blockades in space is less fertile than the discussions of blockades in other domains for two reasons. First, space is open to all, but the high costs of entry to the domain reduce the number of actors operating in space. Second, space is used primarily for commercial use, and weapons have not yet accompanied power (although many of the commercial systems are capable of being weaponized).[116] As a result of these factors and fear of a space arms race, traditional blockades and other types of wartime operations have not yet been implemented in space.

However, some security analysts argue that space is being weaponized in subtle ways and should not be treated differently from any other domain. They argue that it is reasonable for a country like the United States to use weapons to deny another country's wartime use of space, just as it would deny their use of land, sea, or air. If space truly is like the other domains, then it is only a matter of time before it will be militarized.[117]

Another unique aspect of space is territorial ownership because space cannot be considered part of the national territory of any country. Without territorial ownership, states cannot construct "blockades" in the traditional sense in space because states do not own parts of space, thus there is no specific territory for which to deny entry or exit. A blockade in space would require states to prevent one another's physical access into the domain, which is possible but may be likely to occur as the result of embargoes, sanctions, or other political or economic measures that impede the acquisition of certain technology, as opposed to military operations that interfere directly with vessels as they attempt to enter space.

Similarly, cyberspace has physical infrastructure that falls within the territorial boundaries of states and can be subject to laws governing territoriality. However, territorial jurisdiction can be considered virtually nonexistent for information transiting through cyberspace because of the speed at which it passes through national boundaries. The nearly instantaneous communications of cyberspace make it difficult to hold states accountable for information that passes through their territory but does not originate or end there.

Information Blockades

Blockades are traditionally employed in physical domains against physical targets, but there is historical precedent for action that may be understood as "information blockades." The term *information blockade* refers to deliberate actions designed to control or prevent the transmission beyond national boundaries (ingress or egress) of information useful to the enemy or its war-making capabilities. This type of blockade has direct relevance for cyber blockades because the goals are the same; cyber blockades involve denying access to information that is available through the technologies of cyberspace in order to achieve political ends.

Information blockades have been a part of warfare since at least the Spanish-American War in 1898, although they were not called blockades at the time.[118] These early informational blockades have important implications for a modern cyber blockade. Some scholars even argue that it was the struggle for control over worldwide communication—specifically undersea cables—that made World War I truly global.[119] In 1945, international legal scholar Charles Cheney Hyde wrote, "Inasmuch as submarine trans-oceanic cables are an agency for the transmission of intelligence throughout the world, their treatment in time of war is a matter of concern to the entire society of nations."[120]

During the Spanish-American War, submarine cables connecting neutrals to territory controlled by the enemy were "not infrequently cut by the naval forces of the United States."[121] Telegraph cables connecting two enemy territories were considered acceptable targets for cutting, as were cables that connected the enemy with neutrals because they could be used for hostile dispatches. International law dictated that these cables could be cut within the territorial waters of the enemy or on the high seas, but not within the territorial waters of a neutral. Although the belligerent had a right to interrupt service during times of war, it could not confiscate the cables (if privately owned) and had to permit resumption of service to neutrals upon the establishment of peace.[122]

The strategic importance of international radio and submarine telegraph cable networks was a critical part of the war offensive on both sides during World War I. The overarching goal of the British offensive was to isolate Germany militarily, politically, and economically. Germany also recognized the importance of cables to effective coalition warfare, and both sides took steps to destroy their opponent's communications links as part of their war-fighting strategy. Eventually successful at destroying German cables, Britain forced the Central Powers to use the Allies' wireless cables to reach beyond Europe and then used interception and cable censorship as part of an informational blockade, compounding the effects of the traditional maritime blockade.[123]

During World War I, cables were increasingly vulnerable to disruption from damage and disrepair due to the implicit threat of submarines that deterred repair ships from conducting routine cable maintenance or emergency repairs, the real threat of submarine attacks on the cables themselves, and the volume of traffic on the cables. At the time, the United States relied heavily on British cables for overseas communication and realized that regardless of its stake in any future war, the structure of the global cable and radio network and the nation's dependence upon lines of communication controlled by other powers placed the country at a distinct disadvantage. As a result, US officials made efforts to protect and expand the nation's international communications infrastructure in support of changing diplomatic, military, and commercial ambitions during the war.[124] The United States began to move from the periphery of the global network to the center and to develop policies to govern and protect the use of this network.

The United States created a permanent executive authority over cable landings on US territory in 1921; the Cable Landing License Act was designed to protect US strategic interests and open the international cable network to competition. However, this act did not designate a central authority for governing or coordinating private-sector cable and radio development with national security needs. According to historian Jonathan Reed Winkler, this failure "stemmed in part from the differing frames of reference the military, the State Department, and the cable and radio companies used when thinking about communications with the rest of the world and the problem of integrating those worldviews." He added, "Such a disconnect was not unique to the question of strategic communications, however, and was symptomatic of a larger problem of coordinating policy and strategy among the army, navy, State Department, Congress, and others concerned with national security, a problem that would become particularly acute in the 1930s."[125]

Submarine cables continued to play an important role in conflict after World War II.[126] Today, cyberspace and the internet are the latest attempt to organize the world's communications networks in ways that will be redundant and survivable and link places of strategic and commercial importance. We face many of the same challenges as before, plus new ones.[127]

As cyber technology becomes more integrated into political and social life, less attention is paid to the social and political dimensions of technology itself. The disparity between societies linked to the network of instantaneous communications and those that are not is significant, and we do not yet understand fully the implications.[128] Neither do we understand the implications of abruptly moving from "linked" to "unlinked" status, such as with a cyber blockade.

Defining Cyber Blockades

A driving question of this research is, what are cyber blockades, and how are they similar to and different from historical blockades? The analysis of historical blockades reveals several important similarities that unite blockade operations across time and different domains and provide a core set of commonalities that define blockade operations. These commonalities are actions undertaken to create a blockade, actors, capabilities, presence of preexisting conflict, and the role of neutrals. This analysis shows consistency in blockades in different domains, despite the unique attributes and technologies associated with each domain. Table 3.1 displays the core similarities and defining features of blockades in different domains.

Proposal of a Preliminary Theory of Cyber Blockades

A preliminary theory suggests that blockades must involve states or similar entities subject to international law. The actors must possess the capabilities and knowledge required to enforce the blockade. Effective enforcement of blockades is critical in the Law of Armed Conflict. Without effectiveness, blockades are not considered valid. Blockades also occur within the context of extant conflict, but they are not necessarily acts of war per se because they can also be used for pacific blockades or punitive measures. The basic actions of blockades, to prevent ingress or egress from a specific geographic area, remain consistent in every domain, and blockades continue to be impartial with respect to the rights of neutrals.

This preliminary theory also suggests that there are several contributing factors to the decision to employ blockades. Actors employ blockades because they have the capabilities to exploit specific vulnerabilities, such as geography and interconnectedness, making certain adversaries more attractive targets for blockades, and potentially to render the blockade more damaging. Blockades allow actors to achieve certain goals, such as to

Table 3.1 Similarities among Blockade Operations in Five Different Domains

	Maritime	Aerial	Land	Space	Informational
Actions	Prevent ingress/egress of ships or craft from ports or harbors	Prevent aircraft from entering an airspace or NFZ	Prevent entry to or exit from a specific city or region	Prevent entry into outer space	Prevent the transmission of information beyond national borders
Actors	States, independent territories	States, independent territories	States	States	States
Capabilities	Superior maritime capabilities; knowledge of the domain and opponent's vulnerabilities	Superior aerial capabilities; knowledge of the domain and opponent's vulnerabilities	Superior land capabilities; knowledge of the domain and opponent's vulnerabilities	Superior technological or economic capabilities; knowledge of the opponent's vulnerabilities	Historically, sea-based capabilities to interfere with cables; knowledge of the domain and opponent's vulnerabilities
Presence of Conflict	War or extant conflict	War or extant conflict	War	War or extant conflict	War
Role of Neutrals	Rights protected	Rights protected	Rights protected	Rights protected	Rights protected

create financial constraints, isolate the adversary politically, create discomfort for society in order to influence political decision making, and demonstrate power and capabilities in the international system. In certain situations, blockades can also be tools of retribution and punishment for real or perceived injustices. There are many tools that actors have at their disposal, but there are clear alternative actions that can achieve the same results with the same associated costs or advantages.

Cyber blockades should share the features and contributing factors of blockades of other domains. These commonalities have historically united blockades across time and different domains; therefore, one would expect them to be present in blockades in cyberspace also. Yet, cyberspace differs from other domains in important ways that must also be considered.

Different domains and time periods have used technology and resources to employ blockades as effectively as possible, which has led to some differences in blockade operations. These differences may be factors in how blockades are constructed in cyberspace. The primary differences among blockades have been the following: the nature of blockades based on the specifics of the domain; types of resources required to construct a blockade; vulnerabilities associated with the domain, its technologies, and the opponent; and the effects of the blockade on the state and society. Based on the literature of international relations theories and cyberspace, one can anticipate that anonymity, cost, and speed of action in cyberspace will present new dimensions for analysis, as they are advantages for cyber blockades that have not been present in historical blockade operations. Finally, international relations theory addresses the relationship among and between actors at different levels of analysis; cyber blockades will likely involve different levels of analysis as individuals and small groups are newly empowered to take action against states. The analysis of cyber blockades in the following chapters examines the relevance of these criteria and contributing factors for blockades in cyberspace.

Notes

1. Lambeth, "Airpower, Spacepower, and Cyberpower," 172.
2. Ibid., 173.
3. Mahan, "Blockade in Relation to Naval Strategy," 863.
4. Barnett, "Technology and Naval Blockade: Past Impact and Future Prospects," 91.
5. Ibid.
6. The Manual on International Law Applicable to Air and Missile Warfare defines exclusion zone as "a three dimensional space beyond the territorial sovereignty of any State in which a Belligerent Party claims to be relieved from certain provisions of the law of international armed conflict, or where that Belligerent Party purports to be entitled to restrict the freedom of aviation (or navigation) of other States." For more information and a broader discussion of the differences between zones and blockades, see Program on Humanitarian Policy and Conflict Research at Harvard University, "Commentary on the HPCR Manual on International Law Applicable to Air and Missile Warfare," 235.
7. I offer a profound thank-you to international law expert Professor Dr. Wolff Heintschel von Heinegg for elucidating the differences between zones and blockades, and their applicability to cyberspace.
8. Parmelee, *Blockade and Sea Power: The Blockade, 1914–1919, and Its Significance for a World State*, 7.
9. Ibid., 8.
10. Ibid., 16.

11. Ibid., 19.

12. Ibid., 21.

13. Long-distance blockades were the policy of controlling/regulating the flow of goods through adjacent-neutral territory, thus eliminating the need for a close-cordon blockade of the traditional type. Medlicott, *The Economic Blockade*, 4–5.

14. Hyde, *International Law, Chiefly as Interpreted and Applied by the United States*, 2100.

15. Ibid., 2100–03.

16. Symonds, *The Civil War at Sea*, 32.

17. Ibid., 33.

18. Ibid., 36.

19. The doctrine of continuous voyage had been debated and discussed since the mid-eighteenth century, but it was not formally established until the US Civil War. Hyde, *International Law, Chiefly as Interpreted and Applied by the United States*, 2130.

20. Siney, *The Allied Blockade of Germany, 1914–1916*.

21. Symonds, *The Civil War at Sea* 58, 170.

22. Parmelee, *Blockade and Sea Power: The Blockade, 1914–1919, and Its Significance for a World State*, 22.

23. Guichard, *The Naval Blockade, 1914–1918*, 13.

24. Medlicott, *The Economic Blockade*, 10; Hyde, *International Law, Chiefly as Interpreted and Applied by the United States*.

25. Guichard, *The Naval Blockade, 1914–1918*, 10.

26. Ibid., 14.

27. Ibid., 47.

28. Ibid., 101–2.

29. Ibid., 103, 311.

30. Parmelee, *Blockade and Sea Power: The Blockade, 1914–1919, and Its Significance for a World State*, 245–6.

31. Crowe, "Memorandum on the Present State of British Relations with France and Germany."

32. Siney, *The Allied Blockade of Germany, 1914–1916*.

33. Guichard, *The Naval Blockade, 1914–1918*, 308–12.

34. Medlicott, *The Economic Blockade*, 2–3.

35. Ibid., 1–44.

36. Ibid., 17.

37. Ibid., 23.

38. Baer, *One Hundred Years of Sea Power: The U.S. Navy, 1890–1990*, 323.

39. Scheinman and Wilkinson, *International Law and Political Crisis: An Analytic Casebook*, 193.

40. Baer, *One Hundred Years of Sea Power: The U.S. Navy, 1890–1990*, 382; White, *The Cuban Missile Crisis*.

41. Scheinman and Wilkinson, *International Law and Political Crisis: An Analytic Casebook*, 181.

42. Baer, *One Hundred Years of Sea Power: The U.S. Navy, 1890–1990*, 387–89.

43. Cdr. Mark D. Hamilton, USN, "Blockade: Why This 19th Century Nelsonian Tool Remains Operationally Relevant Today," (Naval War College, 2007), 7–8.

44. Bruce A. Elleman and S. C. M. Paine, *Naval Blockades and Seapower: Strategies and Counter-Strategies, 1805–2005*, Cass Series—Naval Policy and History (London; New York: Routledge, 2006), 175–79.

45. United Nations Security Council, "Security Council Resolution 665 (1990)." For more information about the embargo, see UNSCR 661 passed on August 6, 1990.

46. Pace, "Confrontation in the Gulf; U.N. Call on Navies to Block Iraq's Trade; Resolution Permits Use of Force, U.S. Says."

47. Baer, *One Hundred Years of Sea Power: The U.S. Navy, 1890–1990*, 448–50.

48. United Nations Security Council, "Security Council Resolution 1973 (2011)." For more information on the embargo, see UNSCR 1970, passed on February 26, 2011.

49. Eshel, "NATO Takes Control—Coordinating Air and Naval Blockade on Libya."

50. de Muth, "Israel's Own Goal: Susan De Muth Looks at the Truth behind the Israeli Media Hype Concerning the Gaza Flotilla Blockade, the Action That Saw a Turning of the Tide of World Opinion"; United Nations Relief and Works Agency for Palestinian Refugees, "2012 U.N.W.R.A. Emergency Appeal."

51. Palmer, "Report of the Secretary-General's Panel of Inquiry on the 31 May 2011 Flotilla Incident."

52. MacFarquhar and Bronner, "Report Finds Naval Blockade of Israel Legal but Faults Raid."

53. United Nations Office for the Coordination of Humanitarian Affairs, "Easing the Blockade—Assessing the Humanitarian Impact on the Population of the Gaza Strip."

54. De Seversky and Rouben Mamoulian Collection (Library of Congress), *Victory through Air Power*; MacMillan, "Air Blockade: What Are Its Possibilities and Difficulties?"

55. For more information on an early vision for air blockades, see "Air Blockade: What Are Its Possibilities and Difficulties?" by Norman MacMillan, http://www.flightglobal.com/FlightPDFArchive/1940/1940%20-%202023.PDF.

56. Douhet, *The Command of the Air*, 3.

57. De Seversky and Rouben Mamoulian Collection (Library of Congress), *Victory through Air Power*, 3.

58. Douhet, *The Command of the Air*, 6.

59. De Seversky and Rouben Mamoulian Collection (Library of Congress), *Victory through Air Power*, 128.

60. Ibid., 128–29.

61. Ibid., 129.

62. Ibid., 130.

63. It could be argued that many no-fly zones also establish de facto aerial blockades along the international perimeter of the exclusion zones.

64. In 1996, it was changed to the thirty-third parallel.

65. United Nations Security Council, "Security Council Resolution 688 (1991)."

66. The United States, United Kingdom, France, and Saudi Arabia deployed military forces in support of Operation Southern Watch. In 1997, France suspended its participation in the NFZ, stating that the operation had lasted too long and was ineffective. In 2001, US and UK forces increased attacks on Iraqi targets in what was later identified as Operation Southern Focus, a precursor to the invasion of coalition forces. The operation

and regular combat engagements continued until 2003, when coalition forces invaded the country and overthrew the government.

67. US Central Command, "Full Organization Authority Record."

68. Regional Headquarters of Allied Forces Southern Command (NATO), "AFSOUTH Factsheet: Operation Deny Flight."

69. Ibid.; United Nations Security Council, "Security Council Resolution 816 (1993)."

70. Regional Headquarters of Allied Forces Southern Command, "AFSOUTH Factsheet: Operation Deny Flight."

71. Martel, *Victory in War: Foundations of Modern Strategy*, 264.

72. Beale, "Bombs over Bosnia: The Role of Airpower in Bosnia-Herzegovina." References provided by "Operation Deny Flight" on Wikipedia.

73. Knesset, "The Second Lebanese War."

74. *USA Today*, "Lebanon Air Blockade Lifted; Naval Blockade Stays in Place for Now."

75. Knesset, "The Second Lebanese War."

76. United Nations Security Council, "Security Council Resolution 1973 (2011)."

77. Daalder and Stavridis, "NATO's Success in Libya."

78. *Economist*, "No Fly Zone in Libya: Will It Work?"

79. North Atlantic Treaty Organization, "NATO and Libya—Operation Unified Protector."

80. *Telegraph*, "NATO Ends 'Most Successful' Libya Mission."

81. US Department of Defense, "Joint Publication 1-02."

82. Slim, *Killing Civilians: Method, Madness, and Morality in War*, 103–4; Kern, *Ancient Siege Warfare*.

83. Kern, *Ancient Siege Warfare*.

84. Ibid., 5.

85. Slim, *Killing Civilians: Method, Madness, and Morality in War*.

86. Gouré, *The Siege of Leningrad*, x.

87. Ziemke, "Siege of Leningrad."

88. "Siege of Leningrad," in *Encyclopædia Britannica Online*.

89. Gouré, *The Siege of Leningrad*, 3, 14.

90. Ibid., 139.

91. Ibid., 127.

92. Ibid., 142.

93. Wikipedia, "Siege of Leningrad." Referencing Adolf Hitler, "Directive No. 1601" (in Russian) and N. I. Baryshnikov (2003), Блокада Ленинграда и Финляндия 194–44 [Finland and the siege of Leningrad], Институт Йохана Бекмана.

94. International Military Tribunal, *Nuremberg Trial Proceedings Vol. 8*, Sixty-Fifth Day, February 22, 1946.

95. Gouré, *The Siege of Leningrad*, 94.

96. Ziemke, "Siege of Leningrad."

97. Salisbury, *The 900 Days: The Siege of Leningrad*, 568.

98. Kern, *Ancient Siege Warfare*, 354; Hyde, *International Law, Chiefly as Interpreted and Applied by the United States*.

99. Scheinman and Wilkinson, *International Law and Political Crisis: An Analytic Casebook*, 36.

100. Miller, *To Save a City: The Berlin Airlift, 1948–1949*, 4.

101. Ibid., 6–7.

102. Ibid., 19.

103. Ibid., 31.

104. Ibid., 32.

105. Ibid.

106. Ibid., 33.

107. Ibid.

108. Ibid., 52–53.

109. Ibid., 54.

110. Ibid.

111. Ibid., 186.

112. Ibid., 187.

113. US Department of Defense, "Joint Publication 1-02."

114. Conversations with senior US Army officers have confirmed that the Army does not conduct blockade operations on land. Interdiction operations appear to be the closest parallel operation, but as discussed, these have important differences in scope, intent, and impact. As a result, it is reasonable to conclude that modern armies do not engage in blockades on land.

115. Pfaltzgraff, "International Relations Theory and Spacepower," 43–51.

116. Krepon, Hitchens, and Katz-Hyman, "Preserving Freedom of Action in Space: Realizing the Potential and Limits of U.S. Spacepower," 120.

117. O'Hanlon, "Balancing Us Security Interests in Space," 137–52.

118. Hyde, *International Law, Chiefly as Interpreted and Applied by the United States*, 1954–58.

119. Winkler, *Nexus: Strategic Communications and American Security in World War I.*

120. Hyde, *International Law, Chiefly as Interpreted and Applied by the United States*, 1956.

121. Ibid., 1955.

122. Ibid., 1954–58.

123. Winkler, *Nexus: Strategic Communications and American Security in World War I*, 267.

124. Ibid., 268–77.

125. Ibid., 273.

126. In 1971, Operation Ivy Bells was the covert US operation to tap into Soviet cables in Soviet territorial waters in order to record and transmit unencrypted messages. The operation was incredibly risky, but it succeeded, undetected, for a decade. This, however, was not a blockade, but rather a form of espionage using the modern information and telecommunications infrastructure. For more information, see Sontag, Drew, and Drew, *Blind Man's Bluff: The Untold Story of American Submarine Espionage*.

127. Winkler, *Nexus: Strategic Communications and American Security in World War I*, 279.

128. Rosa and Scheuerman, *High-Speed Society: Social Acceleration, Power, and Modernity*; Morozov, *The Net Delusion: The Dark Side of Internet Freedom*.

CHAPTER 4

Cyber Attacks on Estonia

"In the very near future many conflicts will not take place on the open field of battle, but rather in spaces on the Internet, fought with the aid of information soldiers, that is hackers. This means that a small force of hackers is stronger than the multi-thousand force of the current armed forces."

> —Nikolai Kuryanovich, Russian State Duma deputy and member of the Security Committee, in 2006 letter of appreciation to hackers against Israeli websites, www.georgiaupdate.ge

Introduction

The cyber attacks on Estonia in April and May of 2007 were unprecedented in their scope and intensity. They were the first widespread distributed denial-of-service (DDoS) attacks to target the government and key services and industries of a nation-state and, as a result, they are frequently referred to as the first cyber war.

The cyber attacks on Estonia prevented major sectors of the Estonian government and economy from conducting daily business using the internet or cyberspace. During the attacks, a large portion of the country could not use cyberspace to send or receive information from beyond its national borders. These attacks degraded the state's capabilities and capacity to respond to internal and external threats. Because of this, they appear to fit the description of cyber blockades.

This chapter investigates whether the Estonia case qualifies as a blockade according to the definition and theory set forth in the preceding chapters,

< 69 >

identifies how it may differ from previous blockades and the preceding theory, and extrapolates from this case in order to identify the conditions under which blockades may occur in cyberspace.

This chapter begins with a justification of why this case is important in international relations research. Next, it provides information on Estonia's current social and political environment as context for understanding the issue of identity politics in Estonia and the polarization of war monuments there. Then it describes the cyber attack on Estonia, detailing the specific events and circumstances of the cyber attack, how it occurred, and the government's response. Next, it examines the cyber attacks' effect on the Estonian government, economy, and society and the response of the international community. Finally, it analyzes these facts in the framework of the theory of blockades presented in preceding chapters.

Case Justification

The cyber events in Estonia in 2007 were the first time a state in its entirety was directly targeted in a massive DDoS attack. This is a prototypical case of how massive cyber attacks can affect state power and capability during a time of peace. As the first widespread DDoS attack designed to deny a state's access to cyberspace, it can be considered a case of cyber blockade with prototypical characteristics and intrinsic importance. The cyber attacks in Estonia and the responses to them shaped international understanding of potential cyber vulnerabilities, warfare, and blockades.

The Estonian case also presents a real policy and security problem for which governments and organizations around the world must prepare. Current international efforts to reach consensus on cyber conduct were spurred, in part, by the attacks on Estonia and the vulnerabilities and lack of consensus revealed by those events. International organizations and governments observed and assisted in responding to the attacks and then began to create policies to address their own security shortfalls. The Estonia case has been examined in books and scholarly articles from many different perspectives. As a result of the prototypical nature, policy implications of the cyber attacks, and overall relevance, these cyber attacks were the subject of significant research and scrutiny. For this reason, it is also a data-rich case.[1]

Background Information on Estonia

Just as cyberspace cuts across other domains, it also is embedded in the local, regional, and global political, social, and economic environment, much of which is socially constructed through shared experience. In order to understand the circumstances of the cyber attacks in Estonia, we must examine the broader context of the attacks, including the historical context.

Located in the northeastern corner of continental Europe, Estonia borders Latvia to the south, the Gulf of Finland and Baltic Sea to the north and west, and Russia to the east. It is a small country of approximately 45,000 square kilometers. The flat, wooded country is home to almost 1.3 million people, 68 percent of whom are ethnic Estonians and 25 percent are ethnic Russians.[2]

Since achieving independence from the Soviet Union in 1991 and the withdrawal of Russian troops in 1994, Estonian politics have looked westward.[3] Estonia joined the European Union and NATO in 2004 and adopted the euro as its currency in January 2011. Estonians participated in NATO operations in Afghanistan and Iraq, as well as antipiracy operations off the coast of Somalia and peacekeeping missions around the world. Estonia also hosts the NATO Cooperative Cyber Defense Center of Excellence in Tallinn.[4]

After independence, the Estonian government built a democratic society and free-market economy around Web-based services right at the time internet technology began to boom. Today, Estonia is one of the most wired countries in the world and enjoys one of the highest levels of per capita income in Eastern Europe and the Baltic States. The country has strong electronic and telecommunication sectors and was the first country in the world to conduct elections online. Estonians perform nearly 98 percent of their banking online, doctors store medical information online, and the police and courts use online case-management systems. It is home to the internationally popular internet phone and video chat program Skype.[5] At the time of the cyber attacks in 2007, approximately 66 percent of Estonians had access to the internet—among the highest percentages of any country in the world at that time.[6]

Language policies have created tensions between Estonia and Russia. Estonian is the official language, and Estonia's citizenship policy requires individuals to either prove citizenship before 1940 or pass an Estonian language competency exam. Ethnic Russians, or Russian-speaking Estonians, many of whom arrived during or after World War II, have integrated into Estonia with varying degrees of success.[7] In the western regions of Estonia, Russians learn Estonian from an early age and usually speak it fluently, whereas in the eastern areas there is a higher concentration of Russian speakers, so Estonian language capability is not necessary for daily life.

Nevertheless, the language requirement remains a barrier to citizenship in Estonia, and many ethnic Russians are stateless people as a result of this policy. Russia accuses the Estonian government of committing human rights violations and using the language requirement to discriminate against the Russian minority.[8] Estonia's population affairs minister views it differently: Russians who speak Estonian have an advantage in the job market because they are multilingual.[9]

Roots of Identity Politics in Estonia

In 1919, Estonia gained its independence from the Russian Empire and remained an independent state until the secret protocol of the Nazi-Soviet Non-Aggression Pact of August 23, 1939, which paved the way for Soviet military occupation and assimilation of Estonia into the USSR in June 1940.[10] During World War II, Estonian soldiers were forced to fight on both the Soviet and German sides of the war. Estonia was occupied first by the USSR for one year, then by Nazi Germany for three years. According to one veteran, the circumstances of geography made Estonia's participation in the war inevitable: "Every Estonian only had one decision to make: whose side to take . . . the Nazis' or the anti-Hitler coalition's."[11] Given the historical relationship with Russia and fears of further conquest, the decision was not easy. During the course of World War II, Estonia suffered three successive occupations by two of the bloodiest regimes in history.[12]

When Nazi German troops arrived in Estonia in 1941, they were greeted by some as liberators from illegal Soviet occupation. In that one year of Soviet occupation, Estonia had suffered greater losses than it did in the subsequent three years of Nazi rule.[13] German forces occupied Estonia until 1944, when Soviet troops "liberated" Tallinn from German rule and reoccupied Estonia and incorporated it into the USSR. According to scholar William Ashmore, "from 1940 until they regained their independence in 1991, Estonia viewed Russia's presence as an illegal occupation. Mass deportations were made, people were summarily executed, and the population was resettled by ethnic Russians. Russians, on the other hand, viewed the Estonians as ungrateful because they were saved by Russians from the Nazi German fascists."[14] Under Soviet occupation, Estonians who had fought on the German side of World War II were imprisoned or executed for treason, since the Soviet Union considered Estonia to be part of the USSR since 1940.[15]

After Estonian independence was reestablished in 1991, Estonia was an ethnically, linguistically, and culturally divided society. Many of the Russians who resettled in Estonia after World War II never learned the Estonian language and thus could not earn Estonian citizenship; they became a socially marginalized minority within Estonia.[16] The bigger difference between ethnic Estonians and Russians involved their contending views of history: ethnic Estonians overwhelmingly believe they were the victims of illegal Soviet occupation from 1944 until 1991, whereas ethnic Russians believe that Estonia voluntarily joined the USSR in 1940 and was truly liberated again in 1944. This disagreement frames the larger debate about identity and politics in modern Estonia.[17]

Conflict of Monuments

On April 26, 2007, the Estonian government began relocating the Monument to the Liberators of Tallinn (commonly called the Bronze Soldier monument) and the remains of unknown soldiers buried beneath it from downtown Tallinn to a nearby military cemetery. This action served as a catalyst for a series of events, including riots in Tallinn, attacks on the Embassy of Estonia in Moscow, and massive cyber attacks on Estonian websites and servers. The removal of the statue was not an isolated or impromptu decision, but rather one embedded in the complex institutions of history, culture, language, and politics of Estonia and its neighbor to the east, Russia.

This was not the first time a World War II monument had sparked controversy in Estonia. On September 2, 2004, the Estonian Ministry of Interior sent a team to the city of Lihula to remove a statue honoring those Estonians who fought with the Germans against the Soviets during World War II. This action was met by protests and riots in the town, and Soviet Army memorials were desecrated in Lihula, Tallinn, and other parts of Estonia.[18]

The removal of the Lihula monument sparked protest because it touched on the issue of dueling histories and identities in Estonia; it sparked outrage among ethnic Estonians who took pride in the Estonian "freedom fighters" who resisted Soviet aggression by fighting alongside German soldiers. In their view of history, these Estonians were heroes who fought for a noble cause and had been denied proper treatment under Soviet rule. The relocation of the Bronze Soldier statue in Tallinn sparked similar outrage among ethnic Russians who viewed it as a symbol of the noble sacrifices of the Soviet soldiers who liberated Tallinn from German rule.[19]

Estonian scholars Piret Ehin and Eiki Berg argue that national identity construction has been a source of conflict or tension in Estonia and the other Baltic states for years. The war of the monuments is a physical manifestation of the dueling histories and contending identities in Estonia that are a result of World War II and Soviet rule. These tensions persisted after independence from the Soviet Union, but they went largely unrecognized by governments or institutions that hoped they would simply fade away. These conflicts, much like the "frozen conflicts" in other former Soviet states, have not disappeared because they represent normative constructions of the past and are intertwined with the goals for the future. Estonia has tried to move forward by integrating into the EU and joining NATO, but it has not dealt with the contentious issues of its past.[20]

Further complicating the issue of Estonian national identity is the Russian government's vested interest in preserving and promoting a view of the past that is compatible with its official government history and influencing its neighboring states to do the same. According to Estonia's foreign minister Urmas Paet, Russia seeks to exert its influence in the Baltic states through its large Russian population or economic pressure, such as sanctions or energy exports. He believes this part of Russian foreign policy is linked to its domestic political needs, saying, "Unfortunately we have seen that Russia tries to use Russians in Estonia as a propaganda tool, as a tool to make their own politics."[21] In addition, Russia refused to ratify the Estonia-Russia border agreement of May 2005 because its preamble contained references to restoration of Estonian independence. Thus, Estonia's current relationship with Russia is complicated by the legacy of Soviet rule and Estonia's desire to integrate in Europe and balance Russian influence.

Events Preceding the Attacks

In 2005, on the sixtieth anniversary of Victory Day, which marked the end of World War II, tensions rose between Estonia and Russia. The Estonian president declined an invitation to attend the celebrations in Moscow because it also marked the beginning of Estonian occupation. This led to months of political debate in Estonia and large crowds at the Bronze Soldier statue on Victory Day in 2006. Notably, an ethnic Estonian showed up at the statue waving an Estonian flag and shouting slogans. He was arrested for causing a disturbance; this in turn led to public outrage that the Estonian flag could not be displayed at a Soviet war memorial in Estonia. Small but violent clashes between ethnic Estonians and ethnic Russians followed. The Estonian president vowed to resolve the problem before the next anniversary of Victory Day.[22]

In January 2007, the Estonian Parliament passed two laws, the Protection of War Graves and the Removal of Forbidden Structures, which gave the national government the power to relocate the monument and circumvented Tallinn city officials who objected.[23] In retaliation, the Russian legislature proposed sanctions against Estonia, saying that the legislation was the first step to fascism and glorifying the Nazi past.[24] The months leading up to the May anniversary were marked by contentious debate over the memorial's future. On April 23, 2007, Russia issued an official protest and warned of "most serious consequences for relations between Russia and Estonia" if the plans to move the monument proceeded.[25]

The Cyber Attacks

On April 26, 2007, the Estonian government ordered the commencement of excavation at the site of the Bronze Soldier statue and graves beneath it; the statue was removed in the early hours of April 27, 2007. This sparked demonstrations and riots in Tallinn and the northeastern cities of Johvi and Kohtla-Jarve, complete with demonstrators throwing bottles and stones, waving Russian flags, smashing cars, and setting billboards on fire. The police managed to gain control of the situation by using water cannons and tear gas, but the two nights of violence and looting left one person dead, 150 injured, and 1,000 detained. Russian officials and state-controlled media called Estonia's decision to move the monument "barbarism," "blasphemy," and "absolutely repulsive." The Estonian government justified the move by saying that the location near a busy intersection was not a proper resting place for the bodies.[26]

The first cyber attacks on Estonia began on the night of April 26. Some of the first attacks on the system were simple vandalism of websites, while others were DDoS attacks and ping flood scripts that flooded the system with data requests and rendered many government and corporate sites inaccessible.[27] In the next few days, the attacks targeted and brought down the websites of several daily newspapers as well as those of the president and prime minister. On April 30, Estonian government officials convened an emergency meeting of computer security experts from government agencies, law enforcement, banks, and internet service providers (ISPs) to create a plan for protecting vital internet functions. It began immediately to block traffic by filtering out all Web addresses that ended in *.ru* (the domain name for sites registered in Russia).[28] The same day, the attacks became more sophisticated by employing botnets. On May 2, international ISPs began assisting with Estonian efforts to block malicious data, and the flow of incoming data began to slow. The first wave of attacks was trailing off.[29]

The goal of the attacks appeared to be to block access to websites of the Estonian government, media outlets, and private companies and paralyze their work. According to experts, the first wave of attacks was straightforward and amateurish, although still effective. The second wave of attacks became increasingly sophisticated, requiring greater knowledge and a more sophisticated computer network.[30]

On May 8, Estonian officials and internet experts from other parts of Europe prepared for another round of cyber attacks that they believed would begin the following day. On May 9, Russia's Victory Day, the largest wave of attacks on Estonian internet sites began. According to the lead expert on the Estonian Computer Emergency Response Team (CERT), 4 million packets of data per second bombarded the targets for twenty-four hours. This was approximately 1,000 times the normal flow of data. Fifty-eight separate botnet attacks were launched against Estonia in a single day. The ten largest attacks heaved 95 megabits of data per second at Estonian servers, with each assault lasting for up to ten hours.[31] The cyber attacks continued for another week. The third wave began on May 18, and attacks continued for days but at a diminished pace.[32]

Approximately 1 million unwitting computers around the world were involved, as the attackers created "zombie computers" that launched coordinated attacks on Estonian websites without their owners' knowledge.[33] The huge spike in data forced Estonia's largest bank, Hansabank, to shut down its online banking services. The attacks came from as far away as Peru, Vietnam, and the United States (although most were "zombie" computers coordinated by a few key organizers).[34]

Although zombie computers from around the world participated in the attacks, information technology experts found that instructions on when and how to execute the DDoS attack were posted on Russian-language websites, leading Estonia to accuse Russia of involvement in the attacks.[35] Estonian foreign minister Urmas Paet said that the IP addresses of some of the attacking computers were inside Russian government institutions, including the president's administration.[36]

Some evidence implicated Russian criminal and business networks in the attacks. These networks were allegedly responsible for distributing and controlling the botnets that infected computers around the world and eventually launched the attacks on Estonia.[37] There have been other instances of cyber attacks in which the Russian Business Network (RBN) is suspected of involvement. In particular, it is accused of "renting" massive herds of botnets for a specific length of time in order to conduct attacks. The duration and intensity of the attacks on Estonia match this profile of "rented" botnet herds. According to *Hacker*, a small Russian-language publication that claims to represent the hacker community, the attack was not coordinated by the Russian government and the botnets used against Estonia were dispatched for free, suggesting that this was a matter of national pride, not financial gain.[38]

On May 5, Estonian police arrested a 19-year-old ethnically Russian Estonian man, Dmitri Galushkevich, who was suspected of helping organize the attacks. He was the only person arrested in coordination with the attacks and was later convicted for taking part in the cyber attacks. He was fined approximately $1,600.[39] However, according to cyber security experts, it is unlikely that he was the only person involved in or responsible for the attacks. Specifically, the Russian youth groups Nashi, Young Russia, and Mestniye are widely suspected of involvement in the attacks.[40]

In the midst of the cyber attacks, Russian youth groups in Moscow organized protests outside of the Embassy of Estonia and chanted antifascist slogans. Nashi members surrounded the embassy, which is also the staff residency, effectively holding the diplomats hostage. They tore down the Estonian flag from the embassy in violation of the Vienna Convention on Diplomatic Relations. Nashi has links to the Russian government, and according to some reports, the protesters were paid by the Russian government.[41]

After a six-day siege on the embassy, pro-Kremlin activists stormed into a hall where Estonian ambassador Marina Kaljurand was about to hold a press conference. Her security guards were able to stop the protesters before they reached the ambassador, but the attempted attack represented another breach of the Vienna Convention and prompted the embassy to close.[42] Ambassador Kaljurand issued a statement criticizing the Russian government for "not taking sufficient measures to implement international obligations to guarantee the security of diplomatic missions and consulates."

Furthermore, she accused the Russian government of approving the attacks, since government forces did not try to protect the embassy.[43]

Tensions between Russia and Estonia were high during the crisis. The Russian government criticized Estonia's decision to move the monument, and the deputies of the Russian Duma demanded an immediate response in the area of economic trade and cooperation, including transportation, energy, and finance.[44]

Russia banned heavy commercial traffic over key highway bridges between the countries, claiming that the bridges needed emergency repair work and suspending rail service between St. Petersburg and Tallinn.[45] Russia halted deliveries of oil, petroleum products, and coal to Estonia.[46] Russian officials called for boycotts of Estonian goods, and the media reported that Russian shop owners pulled Estonian goods from their shelves.[47] Russia never formally announced sanctions, but there was a significant decline in trade shortly thereafter. According to experts, these actions fit a pattern of Russian foreign policy that involves cutting energy, transportation, and other links to neighboring states in retaliation for perceived anti-Russian policies.[48]

The Government of Estonia's Response to the Attacks

The DDoS attacks on Estonia's internet infrastructure lasted for a total of twenty-two days, threatening the security of the nation and causing a significant impact on daily life.[49] The cyber attacks prevented access to media and government websites for days, leaving citizens in an information vacuum during a time of crisis. The attacks took down banking websites, leaving citizens unable to access online services; for a nation that conducts 98 percent of its banking transactions online, this is a significant event. The telephone exchanges were taken down for over an hour, jeopardizing emergency response services. The attack impacted everyday activities of Estonians, such as pumping gas, withdrawing money at automatic teller machines, grocery shopping, and using mobile telephones. The attacks affected anyone who used the internet in Estonia, whether they were individuals, businesses, or government.[50] According to Hillar Aarelaid, director of Estonia's CERT, "all major commercial banks, telcos, media outlets, and name servers—the phone books of the Internet—felt the impact, and this affected the majority of the Estonian population. This was the first time that a botnet threatened the national security of an entire nation."[51]

Before the attacks began, Estonia's CERT suspected that a cyber attack might accompany the social unrest caused by the monument conflict. According to Aarelaid, experience had taught them that "if there are fights on the street, there are going to be fights on the Internet."[52] In preparation, Aarelaid erected firewalls around government websites, established extra computer servers, and alerted his staff to the potential for an increased volume of cyber attacks.[53]

When the attacks began, the government of Estonia's immediate response to the attacks was to impose a self-blockade in cyberspace: it closed down sites under attack to external (foreign) internet servers.[54] This step was critical to preventing the malicious attacks from gaining entry, thus preserving the integrity of the national information system. It allowed CERT experts to filter out communications from outside Estonia, in the hopes of preserving access for domestic servers and users.[55] Internet experts in Germany, Finland, Slovenia, and other countries assisted in the effort to track down computers that were involved worldwide and block their access to Estonian servers and sites.[56]

By pure chance, during the attacks there was a meeting in Tallinn of European network operators and the so-called Vetted: the select few individuals who are trusted by the largest ISPs in the world and can request that ISPs kick rogue computers off their networks. Aarelaid met with Kurtis Lindqvist, who is a member of the Vetted and in charge of one of the world's thirteen Domain Name System (DNS) root servers, as well as a few other members; they agreed to make calls on his behalf and join him at CERT headquarters on occasion to help manage the response to the attacks.[57]

The government's second step of the response was to reconfigure Estonian servers to address a critical design flaw. The original design required every website to pull content from a database source to answer every request for the website; the solution was to create back-end databases that could store caches of the websites that could better manage repeated floods of request for the same data. This step was the permanent solution that brought most of Estonia's websites back online within seventy-two hours.[58]

The government managed its response so that the attacks caused only short-term internet outages, and there was no permanent damage to the system or infrastructure. Estonia's highly capable CERT coordinated responses between government and civilian information technology experts. Despite the capable and well-coordinated response to the attacks, the use of fake IP addresses, use of zombie computers, and inherent ambiguity associated with the internet meant that Estonia was unable to determine conclusively who initiated the cyber attacks.[59]

After the attacks subsided and the critical data could be analyzed more comprehensively, it became evident that the attacks were not as sophisticated as originally believed. It is impossible to know the goals of the cyber attacks without identifying the perpetrators, but it appears that the attacks aimed to completely shut down the cyber infrastructure in Estonia. In that respect they failed, but they succeeded in shutting down a significant portion of it for several days, denying Estonians abroad access to government or financial services and forcing the government to impose a self-blockade.

The DDoS method of attack is generally criticized for being a blunt tool in cyberspace; it is the hammer of cyber attacks and therefore does not require the technical sophistication or secrecy of other tools, such as the Stuxnet worm. However, DDoS attacks using botnets have their advantages. The botnets needed to take over a computer can be installed well in advance of their use and without detection. Computers all over the world can be harnessed for botnet attacks, making it exceedingly difficult to trace the source of the attack and presenting complicated legal issues for the countries where the hijacked computers are located.[60]

Effects of the Cyber Attacks

The major effects of the cyber attacks were political, social, and economic. The political effects centered on decreased capability of the state to provide services to its citizens. The fact that the cyber attacks occurred during a period of domestic crisis exacerbated the situation by preventing the states from communicating through normal channels with its citizens during a period of internal unrest. Nonetheless, there is little evidence of permanent political damage to Estonia due to the cyber attacks.

The social effects of the cyber attacks were significant. For the first time, a country's communications infrastructure was attacked and disrupted during peacetime. While the attacks lasted only for a matter of weeks, no one knew that during the events, which led to panic and fear. Given the history of Estonia's relationship with Russia, many Estonians feared that the cyber attacks were the beginning of a campaign of Russian aggression against Estonia.

The economic effects on Estonia were not as profound as they could have been, despite the inconvenience of several major banks suspending online operations. Reliable figures are almost impossible to obtain, since the financial cost of the attacks would be determined by lost economic opportunities. Nonetheless, some experts estimate that the banking sector suffered losses of at least $1 million.[61]

Despite the lack of permanent damage, the significance of the attack was frightening as it revealed the vulnerabilities of the ubiquitous modern communication networks. Media around the world heralded it as the first "cyber war" and a harbinger of future conflicts. Governments across the globe stepped up their efforts to protect their critical cyber systems and infrastructure. Researchers renewed and refocused their work in cyber security technologies and policies, which had been overshadowed by the threats of terrorism in the post-9/11 era.[62]

The distributed nature of DDoS attacks and use of zombie computers made plausible deniability easy for suspected attackers. In the case of Estonia, attribution of the cyber attacks could not be determined decisively, despite the best attempts of Estonian and international IT experts. The only person arrested in connection with the cyber attacks was the ethnic Russian youth in Estonia. However, Nashi claimed responsibility for the attacks in a new report.[63] Nashi receives funding and support from the Russian government but is not officially a part of the government, which presents a problem for those attempting to pin the cyber attack on the Russian government.[64]

International Reaction

Russia

The cyber attacks exacerbated Russian-Estonian relations, which were already strained by earlier political disagreements. The Federation Council of the Federal Assembly of the Russian Federation called the leaders in Estonia who were responsible for the demolition of the monument "radical and neo-Nazi."[65] During the crisis, both houses of the Russian parliament called on Putin to sever diplomatic relations with Estonia.[66] The Russian Duma delegation that visited Estonia called on the democratically elected government of Estonia to resign because of the crisis.[67]

Estonia could not prove Russian involvement in the attacks, but members of the Estonian government (including the Estonian prime minister, Andrus Ansip) believed that Russia was responsible for the cyber attacks and issued several official statements saying that individuals in Russia were responsible. The Russian government adamantly refuted the allegations. Deputy Press Secretary for the Russian President Dmitry Peskov flatly denied involvement, saying, "Russia can no way be involved in cyber terrorism, and all claims to the contrary are an absolute lie."[68]

During the cyber attacks, Estonia invoked its mutual assistance treaty with Russia for help finding the individual or individuals responsible for the attacks, but Russia refused to cooperate and declined to allow investigations of individuals and computers located in Russia. This refusal made an in-depth investigation of the forensic cyber evidence impossible. Combined with the train and commercial traffic embargo and the instructions posted on Russian-language websites, this refusal cast a shadow on Russia's claims of innocence and made it appear complicit, if not culpable, in the cyber attacks.[69]

Two years later during a videoconference between Moscow and Washington, DC, Sergie Markov, a State Duma deputy and member of the Russian delegation to the Parliamentary Assembly of the Council of Europe, stated that the DDoS attacks on Estonia in 2007 were organized by his assistant. He claimed that on May 9, 2007, his assistant—without official government orders—attacked Estonian sites in response to the Estonian government's removal of the statue.[70] It was unclear if this comment was intended as a joke, but it was widely interpreted in the West as a serious admission of responsibility.

European Union

The European Union (EU) sent IT experts to Estonia to observe and assist during the attacks. These international experts were invited by Estonia to help assess the scope of the attacks and the damage caused. In the wake of the attacks, Estonia called for greater EU and NATO cooperation in finding practical ways to defend against cyber attacks.[71]

The government of Estonia viewed the riots and relocation of the monument as domestic problems, but it saw Russian retaliatory actions against Estonia as a matter that concerned the whole EU and therefore requested EU support after the crisis erupted. While the crisis escalated, the Estonian government continued to focus on containing it, but as the situation deteriorated, the Estonian foreign minster declared, "The European Union is under attack, as Russia is attacking Estonia."[72] The foreign minister then began to encourage an EU response to Russia, including postponement of upcoming summits.[73]

Once the crisis was under way, the EU and several member states issued statements of support for Estonia. EU High Representative Javier Solana conducted "telephone diplomacy" with Russia. The European Commission (EC) sent a message through its Moscow delegation urging Russian businesses to honor their contracts with Estonia, even though the EC had little leverage on the issue.[74]

The EU's foreign policy toward Russia has been one of the most divisive issues in the organization. The idea of "EU solidarity" enjoys much support within the EU, but member states strongly contest its implications in practical matters. According to some EU member states, Moscow tries to exploit these disagreements to weaken EU unity and isolate states that have an unfavorable policy toward it.[75]

After the first two nights of riots, German chancellor Angela Merkel had telephone conversations with Putin and Ansip, during which she encouraged both sides to show restraint. She encouraged direct Estonian-Russian contacts, but also acknowledged that the relocation of the monument was a sovereign decision of Estonia and an internal matter. The president of the EC called for a mutual dialogue on the sensitive issue and declared that Estonian problems were a problem for all of Europe.[76]

Days later, when the crisis intensified with attacks on the Embassy of Estonia in Moscow, Merkel urged Moscow to comply with its obligations under the Vienna Diplomatic Convention to protect embassies and their personnel. The European Parliament passed a resolution on the matter and the European Council and European Commission also issued a statement on the situation.[77] Following this, the German foreign minister negotiated that Russian authorities would disperse the crowds in front of the embassy if the Estonian ambassador left the country. When she had done so, Nashi and the other youth groups that had been demonstrating in front of the embassy declared victory.[78]

Although many European countries issued statements of support for Estonia, some reportedly questioned behind closed doors the wisdom of the decision to move the monument. Many governments resented being drawn into a politicized bilateral historical dispute, but nonetheless they remained firm in their decision to support Estonia in the face of threats and pressure from Russia. The fact that Tallinn was restrained in its response to the crisis and exhausted its own resources and political capital with Russia before asking for EU assistance made it appear pragmatic and cooperative, which eased the way for EU support.[79]

North Atlantic Treaty Organization

The cyber attack on Estonia, a member of the North Atlantic Treaty Organization (NATO), generated concern within the alliance. In a phone call to the Estonian president, NATO Secretary General Jaap de Hoop Scheffer expressed concern over the behavior of Russia during the monument crisis, which he described as "an internal matter of Estonia." Scheffer also expressed concern over the cyber attacks that targeted Estonian government institutions.[80] In an official statement, NATO said, "It was a concerted, well-organized attack, and that's why Estonia has taken it so seriously and so have we."[81] In addition, NATO expressed deep concern over "threats to the physical safety of Estonian diplomatic staff, including the ambassador, in Moscow, as well as intimidation at the Estonian embassy."[82]

The cyber attacks raised three serious questions for the alliance. The first major question that came out of the attacks was: Could this happen to other member states? It was quickly apparent that it indeed could happen to them, as well as to intergovernmental organizations, such as NATO, and compromise its effectiveness. According to an official at NATO headquarters in Brussels, "this is an operational security issue, something we're taking very seriously . . . . It goes to the heart of the alliance's modus operandi."[83]

The second major question that arose was: Did the attack qualify as an armed attack or an act of war? The answer to this question was far less clear because no state had extant policy on whether a cyber attack could be considered the equivalent of an armed attack. The Estonian minister of defense said this issue needed to be seriously considered, but at the time of the attack, there was no consensus in NATO with regards to cyber attacks and the invocation of Article 5.[84]

The third major question that sprang from the attack was: If the cyber attack was considered an armed attack, could Estonia invoke Article 5 of the North Atlantic Treaty? Article 5 for collective defense stipulates that the armed attack must originate outside of NATO, meaning that a member state cannot invoke collective defense for an attack launched by actors within a NATO member country.

This was problematic for Estonia because attribution in cyberspace is so difficult and time-consuming that it is unlikely that the attacker will be identified quickly enough to involve NATO and make a difference in the course of events.[85] The difficult and tedious process of attribution in cyberspace will continue to plague governments and alliances' efforts to respond quickly and appropriately to cyber attacks and elevates the importance of denial in cyber attacks. Thus, even if NATO were to classify a cyber attack as an armed attack or an act of war, that would not be sufficient to guarantee a NATO response. Accordingly, NATO was careful not to accuse Russia of participating in the attacks against Estonia, despite Estonia's accusations.[86]

United States

The United States' response to the events in Estonia was swift but not strong. At the time of the crisis, the United States was in a period of cool relations with Russia, as the Russian government had recently likened the Bush administration to Hitler and made other inflammatory remarks.[87] The United States expressed deep concern about the cyber attacks, violations of the Vienna Convention, and unrest in Estonia, but did not become directly involved in Estonia's dispute with Russia.

In terms of practical help, the Federal Bureau of Investigation provided assistance with the cyber attacks, according to Estonian officials.[88] The United States also warned Russia that threats against Estonia had no place.[89] As a member of NATO, the United States was involved in its institutional response to the crisis.

On May 3, 2007, US secretary of state Condoleezza Rice expressed concern over the situation in Estonia and said she hoped that the siege of the embassy in Moscow would end.[90] The next day the US Senate passed a resolution condemning violence in Estonia and the attacks on its embassies and expressing solidarity with the government and people of Estonia.[91] In addition, the US State Department demanded that Russia protect the Embassy of Estonia in Moscow and declared that the monument issue was an internal Estonian matter. Thaddeus McCotter, member of the US House of Representatives, stated, "I rise to defend the sovereignty and national dignity of our friend and ally Estonia, condemn Russia's unwarranted intrusions against these free people, and affirm our commitment to America and Estonia's common cause of human freedom."[92]

Analysis

The facts and circumstances of the Estonia cyber attacks in 2007 provide appropriate information for an analysis of the case based on the theory of blockades presented in the previous chapter. The criteria for analysis are the actions undertaken, actors, capabilities, presence of extant conflict, and role of neutrals. This section also examines the contributing factors of the circumstances or conditions under which cyber blockades are likely to occur, including vulnerabilities, goals of the attacks, and alternative courses of action.

Actions

The cyber attacks sought to prevent the Estonian government, media, and financial organizations from using cyberspace and its associated technologies for the exchange of data and information. The cyber attacks resulted in a cyber blockade that prevented the transmission of information to or from Estonian websites to anywhere in the world. The Estonian government's efforts to save the system and mitigate the effects of the cyber attacks required it to sever Estonia's international cyber connectivity in order to restore and preserve access to cyberspace for essential domestic functions. The cyber blockade isolated Estonia from the global cyberspace domain, and in response Estonia imposed restrictions on its own access to cyberspace, essentially quarantining itself in order to restore and preserve the integrity of the system.

Actors

The actors involved in the case of Estonia were both state and nonstate actors. The state actor was the Republic of Estonia, whose government and financial sectors were targeted for attack. Nonstate actors inside of Estonia, such as individuals and private organizations, were also subjected to the cyber blockade. The perpetrators of the cyber blockades were nonstate actors—groups of individuals who spontaneously took up "cyber arms" against Estonia in retaliation for its decision to move the Bronze Monument. The big question of attribution lies in whether these nonstate actors had support or encouragement from Russia. While it seems likely that the Russian government was involved at least indirectly in supporting the cyber attackers, there is no proof of it. If Russia were involved, it would be a case of a state actor using nonstate actors as proxies in a conflict in order to minimize blowback on the state and maintain plausible deniability.

For the one perpetrator of the cyber attacks who was caught, his motives (if they are to be believed) appeared rational. It is logical and rational that individuals would take action to protest a decision to which they objected and perceived as an offense to their ancestors or ethnic group. For nonstate actors, cyber attacks provide an excellent way to wield a disproportionate effect that is disruptive but not life-threatening (in general) and potentially avoid being caught.

If the Russian government was involved, cyber attacks of this magnitude would also be a rational course of action to punish the Estonian government for its political decisions and demonstrate capabilities that could be used against it in the future. This show of capabilities is a threat unto itself, making Estonia and other nations aware of the possible consequences of undertaking a decision that might offend Russia.

Capabilities

The capabilities necessary to launch a DDoS attack like the one on Estonia included the malware for the DDoS attacks, host sites for the sharing of information, and access to botnet herds. The fact that the cyber attacks tapered off so dramatically at the end of each wave of attack supports the theory that botnet herds were rented out for specific periods of time. Botnet herds can be hired from criminal organizations (such as the Russian Business Network), but renting herds for the duration and intensity of the attacks on Estonia would require a substantial amount of money.

The perpetrators of the cyber attacks against Estonia needed to have the technological expertise to create and distribute the malware that was the basis for the DDoS attacks. They also needed to have the appropriate connections to rent botnet herds on the black market. Finally, the cyber attackers also appeared to have knowledge of Estonia's dependency on information technology and its technical vulnerabilities. Additional foresight or information may not have been necessary in this attack because it had the element of surprise; the Estonian government was probably less prepared for the cyber attack than it might have been if there had been a precedent for this kind of attack.

Preexistence of Conflict

Simmering tensions and political conflict preceded the cyber attacks on Estonia and may be considered a contributing factor to the conflict. Estonia and Russia were not engaged in a violent conflict at the time of the cyber attacks, but they were engaged in a political dispute over Estonian domestic policy regarding its Soviet past and ethnic Russian minority. Russia threatened Estonia with retaliatory measures if it relocated the Bronze Monument, and it employed economic and diplomatic tools to pressure Estonia toward a favorable decision, including breaching the Vienna Convention.

For the ethnically Russian Estonians who were involved in the cyber attacks, there was a history of tension between them and the Estonian government. The issues of citizenship, language tests, and employment and the conflicting narratives of history had been major sources of tension in Estonian domestic politics for years. Tensions between the Russian minority and Estonian government had flared around the anniversary of Victory Day for several years, and these flaring tensions may have led the Estonian government to move the Bronze Monument to a less controversial location.

Because they occurred in peacetime, the cyber attacks on Estonia generated an international discussion about the use of force in cyberspace and the use of technology alongside or as a replacement for traditional types of warfare. In the end, Estonia classified the cyber attacks as criminal activity, but the lessons of the conflict and the definition of "cyber warfare" continue to be discussed in international and national forums. NATO has since decided the cyber attacks can be considered acts of war, although it has not clarified the "red lines" that determine which kinds of cyber attacks and under what circumstances. States are obligated by international treaties to respond to threats and acts of war with no more than proportionate force, but proportionality is unclear in a cyber conflict that affects societies and can have unanticipated consequences. As a result, the debate about acts of war in cyberspace continues.

Rights of Neutrals

The cyber attacks against Estonia specifically targeted Estonian websites and servers. Neutral parties seeking to use cyberspace and its associated technologies to communicate with Estonia were affected to some degree, but they were not the targets of the cyber attacks. The cyber attacks did not degrade the entire system of cyberspace; instead, they impaired the function of one of its nodes of communication. Other countries continued to access cyberspace in the normal, uneventful manner.

Vulnerabilities

Estonia had particular vulnerabilities that may have contributed to the decision to launch a cyber attack against the state. As a state highly dependent on technology, it appeared reasonable that an attack on this technology could have significant impact on the government, financial, and social interactions of the country. Furthermore, the fact that a cyber attack on this scale had never before been launched at a state made it less likely that the Estonian government or private sector would anticipate the attack or undertake preparations for defending their systems. The element of surprise allowed the cyber attackers to exploit vulnerabilities within the Estonian IT system that had been considered normal or routine up until that point. After the cyber attack on Estonia, these vulnerabilities were addressed, and a similar style of attack would not be effective in the future.

One of the IT vulnerabilities of the attack was the way websites and servers were configured. To deal with normal levels of requests, websites sent queries to the server to address every request for the site. This process was appropriate for normal activity levels, but during the cyber attack it caused the server system to overload and crash. As a result, the sites and servers had to be reprogrammed so that sites would display cached results for queries instead of requesting information from the servers every time. This is a relatively minor technological vulnerability, but it allowed the cyber attacks to be successful until it was remedied.

Goals of Attack

The party or parties responsible for the cyber attack on Estonia in 2007 did not issue a statement explaining the goals of the attacks, but the goals may be inferred by the circumstances and conditions under which the attacks occurred. The cyber attacks appeared a direct retaliation for the relocation of the Bronze Monument, and given how quickly the attacks began, they may have been premeditated and preplanned.

The goals of the cyber attacks on Estonia in 2007 appeared social, economic, and political. First, the cyber attacks sowed fear and confusion during a time of domestic unrest, when citizens were demonstrating in cities and rioting in the capital. At the time of the cyber attacks, no one knew how long they would last, what their effects would be, and whether other aggressive actions would follow. The uncertainty surrounding the severity and duration of the attacks caused deep fear and uneasiness throughout Estonia.

Second, the attackers degraded the financial sector in Estonia and caused economic distress. The banking sector was impaired for several days, but it was not in danger of collapse, although that may have been the goal of the attacks. The fact that the financial sector did not suffer more damage was due to the government's and IT experts' capable response to the situation, not necessarily the limited ambition or intentions of the cyber attackers. It seems prudent to assume that the cyber attackers sought to do as much

damage to the IT sector as they could, and the lack of more serious consequences is attributable to the competency of the IT experts who mitigated
the effects of the attacks.

Third, the attackers created chaos in the country and undermined the
Estonian government's ability to control events within the country. The
government's ability to protect its citizens and maintain normal life during
a crisis is important to public perception; the cyber attacks directly challenged the government's ability to maintain stability and normal activities.
This chaos conveniently led to an opportunity for the Russian government
to call for the Estonian government to step down because of its difficulty
in managing the crisis.

Alternative Courses of Action

It is difficult to say what alternative courses of action existed in this case.
For the nonstate actors who perpetrated the attacks, their alternative courses
of action were limited to protests or petitions, neither of which would have
had the same level of impact as the cyber attack (although they would have
had the benefit of legality). Cyberspace allows individuals and nonstate
actors a greater platform for engagement in political affairs, and it appears
that this was the most effective (although illegal) course of action for the
nonstate actors in this situation.

If Russia was involved with the cyber attacks, then it had several alternative courses of action, many of which it employed. Russia imposed economic sanctions on Estonia, most notably by halting railway traffic between
the two countries. In addition, it used several diplomatic tools to reproach
the Estonian government. It issued political threats and violated the Vienna
Convention by allowing assaults on the Estonian Embassy and staff in
Moscow, the Duma called for the Estonian government to resign, and a
delegation of Russian officials traveled to Tallinn to call for the resignation
of the democratically elected Estonian government. Given Russian actions
and threats against Estonia, the cyber attack could be perceived merely as
a continuation of its policy in a different domain.

Conclusion

Estonian minister of defense Jack Aaviksoo likened the cyber attacks to a
blockade, saying, "When the navy of another country blocks a country's

ports or when the air force of another country blocks a country's air space, this is in no way different from blocking access to the web pages of another country with cyber attacks. That cannot be treated as hooliganism, but has to be treated as an attack against the state."[93] Aside from the question of who was responsible for the attacks, the other most pressing question was: How should states respond to attacks designed to sever their connection to cyberspace? What are the legal and ethical recourses available after a massive cyber attack against a state? In May 2007, most states and international organizations could not answer those questions. Estonia itself did not know. After the dust settled and the botnets ceased their invasion of Estonian websites and servers, the Estonian government could not make the case for cyber war (as it was understood at the time) and eventually classified the attack as an act of cyber terrorism.[94]

An analysis of the cyber attack on Estonia in 2007 reveals that it fits the criteria for a blockade in cyberspace. The actions undertaken, actors involved, capabilities, preexisting conflict, and rights of neutrals fit the definition of a blockade in cyberspace. The contributing factors that may have led to the attack, including vulnerabilities, goals of the attacks, and alternative courses of action, also fit the blockade theory.

In addition, the cyber attacks on Estonia differ from other blockades in the ways that one would expect. Given the medium and the unique attributes of the domain, cyber activities such as DDoS attacks are an effective way of constructing a blockade in cyberspace. The resources required for this cyber blockade include specific types of hardware and software, but resources for blockades always depend on the characteristics of the domain. The vulnerabilities of the blockaded country and effects of the blockade are different for cyberspace than for other domains, but this is true for all domains.

The unique characteristics of cyberspace brought out new aspects of the cyber blockade that would not be possible in other domains. Anonymity and plausible deniability were much more important in the cyber blockade against Estonia than would be the case with blockades in other domains. Most of the time, it is relatively easy to know who is imposing the blockade; Estonia did not and still does not know, or is unable to prove, who was responsible for the cyber blockade. The cost of the cyber blockade was relatively low since it only required the renting of botnets for a few weeks. The political cost to the blockading actor could have been higher if its identity were known. Finally, the cyber blockade occurred much faster than a blockade in another domain could have. It is likely that the cyber attacks were preplanned and coordinated, but they did not require months or years of preparation in order to execute. While they only lasted for a few weeks, they lasted long enough to demonstrate the attackers' power and capabilities and create chaos and fear in Estonia.

Notes

1. Van Evera, *Guide to Methods for Students of Political Science*, 88.
2. The remainder of the population is from other northern European countries. US Central Intelligence Agency, "The World Factbook: Estonia."
3. Kasekamp and Saeter, *Estonian Membership in the EU: Security and Foreign Policy Aspects*.
4. US Department of State, "Background Note: Estonia."
5. US Central Intelligence Agency, "The World Factbook: Estonia"; Dumbacker, "Lessons from Estonia: Preparing for a Major Cyberattack"; Goodman, "Cyber Deterrence: Tougher in Theory Than in Practice?," 110–11.
6. International Telecommunications Union, "Percentage of Individuals Using the Internet 2000–2010."
7. For example, in the eastern city of Narva, which is closer to St. Petersburg than to Tallinn, only 3 percent of the population is native Estonian, whereas 83 percent is Russian, and the rest come from other former Soviet states. For matters of practicality, the city is 100 percent Russian-speaking and the public schools are language-immersion schools that teach in Estonian.
8. Roth, "Bilateral Disputes between E.U. Member States and Russia," 12.
9. Jackson, "Russian Roots and an Estonian Future."
10. Despite their independence during this period, one resident British diplomat noted that the lives of Estonians resembled "the lives of the hunted" because they did not have a sense of security. Kasekamp and Saeter, *Estonian Membership in the Eu: Security and Foreign Policy Aspects*, 35.
11. Jackson, "When Giants Fought in Estonia."
12. Kasekamp and Saeter, *Estonian Membership in the EU: Security and Foreign Policy Aspects*, 35.
13. Brüggemann and Kasekamp, "The Politics of History and the 'War of Monuments' in Estonia," 427.
14. Ashmore, "Impact of Alleged Russian Cyber Attacks," 6.
15. Brüggemann and Kasekamp, "The Politics of History and the 'War of Monuments' in Estonia," 428.
16. Jackson, "Russian Roots and an Estonian Future."
17. Brüggemann and Kasekamp, "The Politics of History and the 'War of Monuments' in Estonia," 429.
18. Ibid., 425.
19. Ibid.
20. Ehin and Berg, "Incompatible Identities? Baltic-Russian Relations and the EU as an Arena for Identity Conflict," 9–10.

21. Jackson, "Playing Estonia's Political Cards."

22. Brüggemann and Kasekamp, "The Politics of History and the 'War of Monuments' in Estonia," 434.

23. Roth, "Bilateral Disputes between E.U. Member States and Russia," 13.

24. Rt.com, "Russia to Consider Sanctions against Estonia."

25. Roth, "Bilateral Disputes between E.U. Member States and Russia," 13.

26. Ibid.; Harding, "Protest by Kremlin as Police Quell Riots in Estonia."

27. Ashmore, "Impact of Alleged Russian Cyber Attacks," 7; Nazario, "Politically Motivated Denial of Service Attacks," 165.

28. Finn, "Cyber Assaults on Estonia Typify a New Battle Tactic."

29. Landler and Markoff, "Digital Fears Emerge after Data Siege in Estonia."

30. See appendix for more details of the cyber attack. BBC News, "Estonian Newspaper Says Russian Cyber Attacks Repelled."

31. As a comparison, 90 megabits of data per second is roughly the equivalent of downloading the entire Windows XP operating system every six seconds for ten hours straight. For sources of this information, see Landler and Markoff, "Digital Fears Emerge after Data Siege in Estonia," 165; Nazario, "Politically Motivated Denial of Service Attacks"; Nazario, "Political DDoS: Estonia and Beyond."

32. Landler and Markoff, "Digital Fears Emerge after Data Siege in Estonia."

33. Finn, "Cyber Assaults on Estonia Typify a New Battle Tactic."

34. Dumbacker, "Lessons from Estonia: Preparing for a Major Cyberattack."

35. Landler and Markoff, "Digital Fears Emerge after Data Siege in Estonia."

36. Baltic News Service, "Last Cyber Attacks against Estonia Take Place during Last Night."

37. Goodman, "Cyber Deterrence: Tougher in Theory Than in Practice?," 111.

38. Davis, "Web War One: Hackers Take Down the Most Wired Country in Europe."

39. Goodman, "Cyber Deterrence: Tougher in Theory Than in Practice?," 111; BBC News, "Estonia Fines Man for 'Cyber War' "; Fox News,"Estonia Charges Solo Hacker for Crippling Cyberattacks."

40. Nazario, "Political DDoS: Estonia and Beyond."

41. Rand and Pau, "Paet: Russia Is Attacking EU through Estonia; According to Foreign Minister, Attack Is Virtual, Psychological, and Real, All at Once."

42. McLaughlin, "Estonia Closes Moscow Embassy as President Berates Russia."

43. "Кальюранд: Кремлевская Администрация Атакует Эстонские Сайты" [Kaljurand: The Kremlin administration is attacking Estonian websites].

44. "Заявление Совета Федерации Федерального Собрания Российской Федерации В Связи С Ситуацией Вокруг Памятника Воину-Освободителю В Таллине" [Statement of the Council of the Federal Assembly of the Russian Federation in connection with the situation around the Soldier Liberator monument in Tallinn].

45. Analysis of Estonian railway transport reveals that after April 2007, the volume of international freight hauled on Estonian public railways almost halved when compared with the first four months of the year. Furthermore, freight flows moved to other Estonia's neighboring countries, thus proving the existence of sanctions on Estonia. For more information, see Koppel, "Impact of Russian Hidden Economic Sanctions on Estonian Railway Transport"; Ashmore, "Impact of Alleged Russian Cyber Attacks," 7; Woehrel,

"Estonia: Current Issues and U.S. Policy," 4; Goodman, "Cyber Deterrence: Tougher in Theory Than in Practice?," 111.

46. Roth, "Bilateral Disputes between E.U. Member States and Russia," 13.

47. Ibid.

48. Woehrel, "Estonia: Current Issues and U.S. Policy," 4.

49. Goodman, "Cyber Deterrence: Tougher in Theory Than in Practice?"

50. Dumbacker, "Lessons from Estonia: Preparing for a Major Cyberattack"; Coalson, "Behind the Estonia Cyberattacks."

51. Davis, "Web War One: Hackers Take Down the Most Wired Country in Europe."

52. Landler and Markoff, "Digital Fears Emerge after Data Siege in Estonia."

53. Ibid.

54. BBC News, "The Cyber Raiders Hitting Estonia."

55. Stiennon, *Surviving Cyberwar*, 89.

56. Landler and Markoff, "Digital Fears Emerge after Data Siege in Estonia."

57. Davis, "Web War One: Hackers Take Down the Most Wired Country in Europe."

58. For more information on the specific type of software employed, see Stiennon, *Surviving Cyberwar*, 89–90.

59. Ashmore, "Impact of Alleged Russian Cyber Attacks," 7.

60. Ibid., 8.

61. Landler and Markoff, "Digital Fears Emerge after Data Siege in Estonia."

62. There is a notable gap in the literature on cyberspace between the late 1990s/2000 and 2007/2008. A few scholarly articles were published during that time, but it appears that there was a resurgence of interest in the topic after 2007.

63. Nazario, "Politically Motivated Denial of Service Attacks," 174.

64. *Rediff India Abroad*, "Nashi, Russia's New Military Nationalist Movement."

65. "Заявление Совета Федерации Федерального Собрания Российской Федерации В Связи С Ситуацией Вокруг Памятника Воину-Освободителю В Таллине" [Statement of the Council of the Federal Assembly of the Russian Federation in connection with the situation around the Soldier Liberator Monument in Tallinn].

66. Harding, "Protest by Kremlin as Police Quell Riots in Estonia."

67. Rand and Pau, "Paet: Russia Is Attacking EU through Estonia; According to Foreign Minister, Attack Is Virtual, Psychological, and Real, All at Once."

68. Ashmore, "Impact of Alleged Russian Cyber Attacks," 8.

69. Goodman, "Cyber Deterrence: Tougher in Theory Than in Practice?," 111.

70. "Депутат Госдумы Признался, Что Эстонские Сайты Завалил Его Помощник" [State Duma deputy admitted that Estonian websites were blocked by his assistant].

71. Woehrel, "Estonia: Current Issues and U.S. Policy," 4.

72. Roth, "Bilateral Disputes between E.U. Member States and Russia," 14.

73. Ibid.

74. Ibid.

75. Ibid., 1.

76. Ibid., 15.

77. European Parliament, "European Parliament Resolution on the Situation in Estonia" (May 21, 2007).

78. Roth, "Bilateral Disputes between E.U. Member States and Russia," 15.

79. Ibid.

80. Baltic News Service, "Te—02!.03.05.07 01.10 J.J. US Urges Russia to Back Off in War Memorial Dispute with Estonia."

81. Finn, "Cyber Assaults on Estonia Typify a New Battle Tactic."

82. Baltic News Service,"Nato Makes Statement Backing Estonia in Row with Russia."

83. Traynor, "Russia Accused of Unleashing Cyberwar to Disable Estonia: Parliament, Ministries, Banks, Media Targeted: NATO Experts Sent in to Strengthen Defences."

84. Baltic News Service, "U.S., European Specialists Help Estonia Deal with Cyber Attacks."

85. The type of attack also matters, as DDoS attacks occur more quickly and provide more plausible deniability than other more technical or sophisticated types of attack.

86. Traynor, "Russia Accused of Unleashing Cyberwar to Disable Estonia: Parliament, Ministries, Banks, Media Targeted: Nato Experts Sent in to Strengthen Defences."

87. Ibid.

88. Finn, "Cyber Assaults on Estonia Typify a New Battle Tactic."

89. Woehrel, "Estonia: Current Issues and U.S. Policy," 4–5.

90. Baltic News Service, "U.S. Secretary of State Expresses Support to Estonia."

91. 110th US Congress, "Senate Resolution 187 (110th)" (Government Printing Office, 2007), http://www.govtrack.us/congress/bills/110/sres187/text; Baltic News Service, "U.S. Sentate Passes Resolution of Solidarity with Estonia."

92. Baltic News Service, "U.S. Congressman Rises to Defend Estonia's Sovereignty."

93. Baltic News Service, "U.S., European Specialists Help Estonia Deal with Cyber Attacks."

94. This was also the United States' policy on cyber attacks of this nature at the time. Poulsen, "Estonia Drops Cyberwar Theory, Claims Packets Were 'Terrorism.'"

CHAPTER 5

The Georgia-Russia War

"Cyber-attacks are part of the information war, making your enemy shut up is a potent weapon of modern warfare."

—The editor of the Russian online journal *Cybersecurity.ru*

Introduction

The cyber attacks in Georgia in 2008 were the first time that conventional military invasion was accompanied by a large-scale cyber attack on the government and services of the country being invaded. This unprecedented move linked cyber attacks with political and military operations on the ground. This case is relevant for cyber blockades because the cyber attacks were designed to cut off Georgia's ability to communicate and exchange information using cyber technology within and beyond its borders during a war. As such, it is a good test case for the proposed theory of cyber blockades.

This chapter examines the cyber attacks that occurred in Georgia in 2008, assesses their impact on the state and society, and determines the extent to which the attacks match the preliminary theory and characteristics of cyber blockades. Unlike in Estonia, where a key issue was determining if the attacks were considered an act of war, the cyber attacks in Georgia occurred within the context of warfare and thus provide a different perspective and context for examining the attacks and their implications.

< 96 >

Case Justification

The Georgia cyber events of 2008 were the first time an overt, concentrated cyber attack was synchronized with a military invasion. Russian forces invaded Georgia on four fronts: air, land, sea, and cyberspace.[1] This is a prototypical case of how cyber attacks can be combined with conventional attacks in other domains in order to increase effectiveness during warfare. As such, it is a relevant case for policymakers because it presents a new development for warfare. For these reasons, it is also a data-rich case because the media, scholars, and international organizations have examined it thoroughly to understand the effects of cyber attacks used in combination with conventional forces.

Georgia at the Crossroads of Technology

Georgia is not as technologically dependent as other countries in Europe, such as Estonia. It ranks 74th out of 234 countries in the number of internet addresses, behind developing countries such as Nigeria and Bangladesh. Vital services, such as transportation and power, are not connected to the internet infrastructure as they are in other countries, such as the United States and United Kingdom.[2] In 2008, Georgia had a relatively low internet penetration rate: approximately 8 internet users per 100 people, which reflects a lack of government or private-sector investment in infrastructure capacity and a correspondingly low dependence on (or demand for) IT infrastructure. Despite this overall penetration rate, Georgia is experiencing a rapid rate of growth of internet users: in 2006, the electronic communications sector reported a user growth rate of 81 percent.[3]

The geography of Georgia presents limitations in terms of physical infrastructure. Its land routes for internet infrastructure include Russia, Turkey, Armenia, and Azerbaijan. According to many sources, Georgia is largely dependent on Russia for its cyber connectivity; more cyber infrastructure routes (nearly half) pass through Russia to Georgia than any other single country. Turkey is also a major telecommunications route for Georgia; most of Georgia's 309 internet networks are routed through Turkey or Azerbaijan (although the Azerbaijan links are then sent through Russia).[4] Thus, the geography of the region and limited options for dispersing internet traffic from Georgia render it more vulnerable to disruption or manipulation by a malevolent actor. Russia has direct control over most of the cyberspace infrastructure linking Georgia to the rest of the world.

At the time of the conflict, a fiber optic cable linking Georgia to Bulgaria across the Black Sea was under construction. This connection would eventually dramatically improve the country's internet connectivity, provide the first privately owned fiber optic system available to Georgians, and diminish Russia's influence over Georgian IT infrastructure.[5] Georgia also has recently expressed interest in expanding the Georgia-Bulgaria fiber optic infrastructure facilities to create a joint telecommunications project with Ukraine via the Black Sea.[6]

Georgia is also a key transit area for the major oil and gas reserves in the Caspian Sea. The Baku-Ceyhan pipeline runs through Georgia on its way from Azerbaijan to Turkey. This pipeline is an important source for oil and gas on the international market, particularly because it is one of the few in the region that is entirely outside of Russian control. The completion of the pipeline in May 2005 raised tensions between Russia and Georgia.

History of the Conflict

Georgia is a diverse country with many different religious, linguistic, and ethnic groups inhabiting the same small piece of earth. Most of these groups have coexisted for hundreds, if not thousands, of years. This coexistence has not always been peaceful, but it created a common history that alternated between independence and conquest by the leading empires of the day, most recently by the USSR.[7] Georgia's transition from Soviet rule to independence in 1990 was difficult, and the country experienced high levels of political instability, violence, ethnic conflict, and economic disruption in the wake of independence. Some of these difficulties were caused by political decisions made in Georgia, but some of them were the result of close Soviet and Russian relations with minority groups within Georgia and the political problems this caused for the newly independent state.[8]

The 2008 conflict between Russia and Georgia centered on the issue of South Ossetia's separation or independence from Georgia. From 1991 to 1992, South Ossetia and Georgia went to war over the status of South Ossetia. The South Ossetians were outmanned and outgunned by the Georgians but received overt and covert support from Russia that enabled them to continue fighting. A ceasefire was reached in 1992, whose terms included establishing South Ossetia as an independent region within Georgia.[9] In 1993,

Figure 5.1   Map of Georgia with South Ossetia and Abkhazia. *Wikimedia Commons*

another war was fought between Georgia and the breakaway region of Abkhazia; it resulted in a similar agreement that established Abkhazia as an independent region within Georgia.[10]

Thus, South Ossetia and Abkhazia became autonomous and de jure militarized zones in Georgia on the border of Russia and the Black Sea, respectively. The "frozen conflicts" over South Ossetia and Abkhazia were not stable. They simmered as low-level conflicts for years, flaring up occasionally over events that would otherwise be considered relatively minor. They are entropic conflicts that have the capability to lead to progressive disorder and chaos, if not resolved or managed effectively.

In accordance with an Organization for Security and Cooperation in Europe (OSCE) agreement, peacekeeping forces composed of 500 Russian, Georgian, and South Ossetian troops kept an uneasy peace between Georgians and Russian-supported South Ossetian separatists.[11] Under this new arrangement, Tskhinvali (the capital of South Ossetia) devolved into a smuggler's paradise of stolen cars, booze, women, drugs, weapons, and counterfeit dollars.[12]

South Ossetia enjoys close ties with Russia, and particularly with the Russian region of North Ossetia. Most of the approximately 70,000 South Ossetians are ethnically distinct from Georgians and Russians, and speak their own language, which is related to Farsi. Approximately two-thirds of the South Ossetian budget, or $30 million, comes directly from Moscow, and the ruble is the currency of the region. Almost all South Ossetians carry Russian passports. In addition, Russia's state-owned gas company, Gazprom, has invested heavily in the region by building new gas pipelines and infrastructure that connect South Ossetia with Russia.[13]

Events Preceding the Attacks

Georgia's Rose Revolution in 2003 did nothing to improve relations between Russia and Georgia since the Russian leadership viewed the revolution as a US-orchestrated shift to undermine its influence in the region. Georgia's National Strategic Concept of 2005 made clear its desire to break completely with its past and join the European Union and NATO. This reorientation away from a "South Caucasus" identity and toward a more European "Black Sea" identity threatened Russia's security along its southern frontier. In the following years, tensions mounted as electrical and gas pipelines connecting Russia and Georgia were blown up on the Russian side of the border, Russia imposed embargoes on Georgia, ethnic Georgians were deported from Russia, Russian spies were deported from Georgia, and Russia bombed Georgian territory in 2007.[14]

On February 17, 2008, Kosovo unilaterally declared independence. While this development was marked by celebrations in the streets of Pristina and Geneva and more than ninety UN member states officially recognized Kosovo within two months, Russia strongly objected and declared Kosovo's independence illegal and a dangerous precedent for separatist movements elsewhere, particularly in the former Soviet Union. Russia's increased support for and later recognition of the independence of South Ossetia and Abkhazia was tit-for-tat retaliation for the international community's acceptance of Kosovo's independence.[15]

In April 2008, a Georgian unarmed unmanned aerial vehicle (UAV) was shot down over Abkhazia. The government of Abkhazia immediately claimed responsibility for the incident, saying that Georgia had violated Abkhaz airspace. However, a video surfaced days later showing a Russian MiG-29 shooting down the UAV.[16] This event escalated tensions further, and Russia announced it would send additional peacekeeping forces to Abkhazia. Low-level violence in Abkhazia and South Ossetia was reported during the ensuing weeks. At the end of May, Russia sent more military troops into Abkhazia, allegedly to repair a railway line. Georgia condemned this as an act of aggression and part of a planned military intervention in the country. In early July 2008, the violence in Abkhazia continued and spread to South Ossetia and Georgia; forces on both sides allegedly engaged in military buildups in violation of the terms of the cease-fire.[17]

During this period of escalating tensions, the German government attempted to mediate the ongoing dispute and help Russia and Georgia reach a diplomatic solution to their disagreements. This effort was not strongly supported by other EU states and failed to reach a resolution. Despite the obvious tensions, the EU was unable to broker a solution or prevent the outbreak of war.[18]

On July 19, 2008, a distributed denial-of-service (DDoS) attack targeted the website of the president of Georgia, Mikheil Saakashvili, and rendered it inaccessible for twenty-four hours. Millions of requests flooded and shut down Georgian servers and the president's website. There was no solid proof that Russia was behind these attacks, but the botnet command-and-control server that sent out the instructions was a MachBot controller, a tool favored by Russian botherders.[19] In addition, the server's domain provided seemingly fake registration information, but it did appear to tie back to Russia. According to experts, the servers involved in this short DDoS attack were based in the United States and had come online just a few weeks prior.[20]

The Attacks

The war between Georgia and Russia officially began on August 7, 2008, after several weeks of arguments over the territory of South Ossetia. It began when Georgian troops, in response to Russian provocation, drove into South Ossetia and shelled Tskhinvali. A few hours later, Russian forces entered Ossetia with airpower and armored and motorized infantry forces. The Russian government claimed that its military operation was a reaction against Georgian aggression against Tskhinvali and Russian peacekeepers in the region. In reality, over 8,000 Russian troops were moved into position along Georgia's northern border during the months preceding the attacks, and Abkhazia's foreign minister had made threatening statements in May 2008 that "it [would] take us two days to go on the offensive into Western Georgia and create a security buffer zone."[21] In addition, multiple reports and official interviews with Russian soldiers after the war revealed that Russian infantry, armor, and heavy guns were deployed south of the Roki Tunnel (the official border between Georgia/South Ossetia and Russia) before August 7—evidence that Russian troops began the invasion into Georgia before Georgian troops began the assault on Tskhinvali.[22]

The Russian counterattack was carefully planned and coordinated; given the speed at which Russian forces responded to the attack on Tskhinvali, it was apparent that they were expecting the attack and ready to engage. Most likely, Russian provocation had baited Georgia to begin hostilities. Russia responded by deploying additional combat troops to South Ossetia, conducting bombing raids in Georgian territory, deploying naval forces to construct a maritime blockade of Georgia, and landing marines on the Abkhaz coast. The ground combat operations of mechanized divisions of Russian military and Ossetian militia forces against lightly armed Georgian military led to a swift defeat of Georgian forces. Within twenty-four hours, Russian forces had consolidated their position, gained control of South Ossetia, and forced Georgian troops back over the border.[23]

On August 10, after gaining control of South Ossetia, Russia launched a two-pronged attack on Georgia proper: one assault came from South Ossetia to the Georgian city of Gori, and the other came from Abkhazia and was designed to cut off Tbilisi from its ports. Russia also bombed the military airfields at Marneuli and Vaziani and disabled radars at the civil international airport in Tbilisi. The combined effect of these assaults brought Russian forces within forty miles of Tbilisi and made external reinforcements or replenishments extremely difficult.[24] An official Georgian estimate after the war claimed that the military operations against Georgia required more than 80,000 Russian servicemen, or one-third of its combat-capable land forces. An invasion of this magnitude would have required long-term planning that involved the entire Russian military.[25]

French president Sarkozy negotiated a cease-fire agreement that the countries signed after one week of fighting, but tensions remain high and Russia has since refused to implement several of the terms of the agreement. One particular concession of the agreement has led to further loss of Georgian territory by allowing Russia to establish an 8-kilometer "security zone" below the borders of South Ossetia and Abkhazia.[26] According to some experts, the only reason Russia agreed to the ceasefire was that it believed Georgian president Saakashvili had been so discredited and politically damaged by the war that the Georgian state would weaken and collapse, allowing greater Russian influence in Georgia and the South Caucasus region as a whole.[27] The conflict forced 25,000 Georgians to flee their homes and become internally displaced persons.[28]

During the military invasion, information warfare was important to both sides. Both Russian and Georgian leaders believed that the way the media treated the war was as important as the actions taken on the battlefield. As a result, the ability to control the media and coverage of the events was a significant part of the strategy for victory on both sides.[29] Historically, they engaged in attempts to control the information available to the opposing side, justify their actions and gain approval in the international scene, and generate or maintain support for their military both at home and abroad. Often these types of information wars involve definition and delivery of a particular message, but sometimes they involve denial through the closure of channels of communication.[30]

The cyber assault on Georgia began on the same day as the military invasion and comprised attacks that led to the defacement of public websites and DDoS attacks against several different targets. The defacements were directed at the websites of highly symbolic political and financial institutions, including the president of Georgia (www.president.gov.ge), the Ministry of Foreign Affairs of Georgia (www.mfa.gov.ge), and the National Bank of the Republic of Georgia (www.nbg.gov.ge). The defacements posted photos of Georgian president Mikheil Saakashvili and Adolf Hitler, as well as other twentieth-century dictators.[31] A group of hackers from South Ossetia claimed responsibility for these defacements.[32]

The defacements were relatively minor events compared with the DDoS attacks on Georgia. The DDoS attacks were high-intensity attacks that flooded the systems with an average of 211.66 megabits per second (Mbps). At its peak, the attacks launched 814.33 Mbps at websites. Each attack lasted for an average of two hours and fifteen minutes, while the longest attack lasted for six hours.[33]

The DDoS attacks targeted the websites of fifty-four government, communications, and financial institutions.[34] The government websites attacked included:

- www.parliament.ge, the Parliament of the Republic of Georgia
- www.president.gov.ge, the president of the Republic of Georgia

- www.abkhazia.gov.ge, official website of the government of the Autonomous Republic of Abkhazia
- www.mes.gov.ge, Ministry of Education and Science of the Republic of Georgia
- www.naec.gov.ge, governmental website providing standardized educational tests for students[35]

The news and media sites attacked included:

- www.forum.ge, biggest forum in Georgia
- www.civil.ge, largest Georgian news page in English
- www.presa.ge, Association Press
- www.apsny.ge, news portal
- www.rustavi2.com, private television company
- www.news.ge, news portal in English
- interpress.ge, news portal[36]

Other websites were also hit by the DDoS attack, including:

- www.tbilisiweb.info, news portal
- www.newsgeorgia.ru, news portal
- www.os-inform.com, privately owned media site
- www.kasparov.ru, Web page of Russian opposition party representative
- www.hacking.ge, Georgian hackers' community website
- www.skandaly.ru, Russian news portal[37]

In the financial services sector, Georgia's largest commercial bank's website was attacked (www.tbc.ge). In total, thirty-six major websites were identified as priority targets, including the Supreme Court of Georgia and multinational targets such as the embassies of the United States and the United Kingdom in Tbilisi.[38] Russian media reported that the site "Georgia-online" was almost destroyed in the cyber attacks.[39]

During the attacks, 35 percent (or over 100) of Georgia's internet networks disappeared, some for a long time. Sixty percent of the networks were considered unstable during the attacks. The highest levels of activity occurred on August 8, 9, and 10, which coincided with Russian tanks moving into South Ossetia.[40]

The attacks came from computers around the globe, suggesting one or several botnets were involved in the attacks. The major attacks were also uniform: they were mostly TCP SYN floods, which interrupt the normal process that must occur for packets of information to arrive at the destination point.[41] The repetition of these TCP SYN attacks fills up the connection queue and denies others access to the services.[42] Among IT experts, there was widespread consensus that cyber attacks on Georgia were planned and coordinated from the beginning, unlike with Estonia, where coordination was recognized only in the second wave of attacks.[43]

Russian-language websites, blogs, and forums posted scripts with instructions for attacking Georgian websites, and one site even included a downloadable file with executable software for launching the attacks. Instructions for how to flood Georgian government websites, as well as a list of vulnerable target sites, were available on Russian-language websites, creating what security experts have dubbed a "cyber kill chain."[44] In this respect, the "crowd-sourcing" of attack information and targets on Russian-language sites was similar to the cyber attacks on Estonia the year before. The primary websites responsible for dispersing information for launching cyber attacks were Xaker.ru and Stopgeorgia.ru (which also used "stopgeorgia.info" as a parallel site). Xaker.ru is a Russian hacker forum that encouraged users to go to Stopgeorgia.ru, a private password-protected site, for more information.[45]

Stopgeorgia.ru provided DDoS links and download for malware to be used in the attacks, lists of the websites that had been tested for vulnerability and were designated priorities for attack, and expert advice for novice hackers, all as part of the effort to allow novices the opportunity to participate in the attack. The site became active for the first time the day after the military invasion of South Ossetia commenced. It was protected by a "bulletproof network," which allowed users a great deal of latitude in conducting illegal operations online.[46]

The cyber attacks on Georgia were also innovative. Instead of relying solely on DDoS attacks, which harness thousands of computers to send individual queries to the site and overload it, the attacks on Georgia used "MySQL," a software suite widely used by websites to manage back-end databases. According to IT expert and Project Grey Goose investigator Billy Rios, a key feature (called the "benchmark" feature) in MySQL "allows site administrators to test the efficiency of database queries," thus determining in real time if their attacks are successful. Rios added that in the Georgia conflict, "hackers posted online instructions for exploiting the benchmark feature to inject millions of junk queries into a targeted database, such that the Web servers behind the site become so tied up with bogus instructions that they effectively cease to function."[47] Thus, while DDoS attacks can require thousands of botnets to bring down a website, SQL injections—particularly with "benchmark" features—require only a handful of machines to achieve the same result.[48]

With this innovation, a small number of users, even just one computer, can bring down back-end databases for multiple sites. This unique feature implies that the attackers conducted reconnaissance and planning prior to the cyber attacks. Given that the cyber attacks coincided with the military invasion of Georgia, this raises the question of coordination between the hackers and the Russian government.[49]

In addition to defacement, DDoS, and SQL attacks, Georgian email addresses were spammed with messages and malware. The reported intent of these attacks was to overload both private and government email servers so as to further hinder communication. Publicly available lists of politicians' email addresses were abused for this purpose.[50]

One Georgian report refers to the cyber attacks as a "cyber blockade." This report claims that the attacks were directed by agents within Russia, primarily the Russian Business Network (RBN). It argues that the attacks amounted to a cyber blockade because "[a]ll Georgian Internet traffic was going through Russia, denying Georgia its Internet independence."[51] Furthermore, the report claims, "by examining Internet routes before and after the beginning of the war, it is clear that they were altered either legally or illegally, blocking traffic in and out of Georgia. Some of those routers are known to be under control of the RBN. This can be demonstrated via a comparison of route configuration before and after the war."[52] Russian media coverage also reported an "information blockade" on Georgia, saying that most of the news coverage about the war came from reporting in Ossetia, not Georgia.[53]

Russian media reporting portrays a slightly different set of events. It claims that websites in South Ossetia were the first targets of attacks, including the websites of the (Russian) Information and Governmental Committee.[54] There were also cyber attacks against Russian media websites. According to Russian media reports, Russian news and search portals were inaccessible in Georgia, as well as Russian television channels. According to Russian reporting, the leaders of Georgia were responsible for these attacks on Russian sites.[55]

Russian media also reported youth protests in Moscow. On August 8, 2012, several youth movements such as Nashi, Molodya Gvardiay, Young Russia, Youth Eurasian Union, and Vanguard of Red Youth set up a tent camp in front of the Georgian Embassy in Moscow in order to protest Georgian activities in South Ossetia. The leaders of several of these youth movements signed a statement that urged an "information war" against the Georgian government on all internet websites.[56]

Effects of the Cyber Attacks on Georgia

The government of Georgia responded to the attacks by moving the president of Georgia's websites to Tulip Systems' servers in the United States and the Ministry of Foreign Affairs' website to an Estonian server. The Office of the President of Poland offered its website for the dissemination of information about the cyber attacks on Georgia and helped provide internet access for the government of Georgia.

The Georgian Computer Emergency Response Team (CERT) led the task of attack mitigation in its role of national CERT during the crisis.[57] CERT Poland and France helped analyze IP data and log files. Also, IT specialists from CERT Estonia traveled to Georgia from August 12 to 16 to provide technical expertise and knowledge gained from the Estonian cyber attacks.[58]

The cyber attacks on Georgia limited communication within the government of Georgia, between the government and its people, and between the government and the international community at a crucial point in time. The military invasion of South Ossetia violated Georgia's territorial sovereignty and constituted an act of war on the part of the Russian government, and the cyber attacks limited the Georgian government's ability to react, respond, and communicate effectively during the earliest days of the war. The cyber attacks exacerbated a crisis and limited the ability of the government of Georgia to govern effectively during a war. An unintended consequence of the DDoS attacks may have been to make the Georgian blogosphere more important than it ever had been and more focused on political topics.[59]

The majority of the damage related to the government's ability to provide information. The people of Georgia were deprived of official government and media reporting of events during war. The government of Georgia was unable to provide information to the international community and characterize the events in a way that represented its interest. The cyber attacks essentially silenced the government during the first few days of a military invasion and deprived it of normal means of mass communication.[60]

The cyber attacks also impacted public services in Georgia. After the cyber attacks on the National Bank of Georgia on August 9, the government ordered all banks to cease electronic services. This blackout of electronic banking services lasted for ten days, with all banks fully operational again on August 18.[61]

According to CERT Estonia, the cyber attacks on Georgia cut off services provided by two of the main internet providers in Georgia. United Telecom's router in Georgia was unavailable and inaccessible for several days, and Caucasus Network Tbilisi was flooded with queries. The flood of queries may have also caused a ripple effect that overloaded smaller internet providers with rerouting requests. Further complicating the situation was the fact that physical infrastructure of Caucasus Network ran directly through South Ossetia, which led to physical damage and disconnection of the infrastructure during the conflict.[62]

The financial damages rendered by the cyber attacks on Georgia are difficult to estimate for three reasons. First, as with the Estonia attacks, measuring economic damages of cyber attacks is difficult because it involves measuring a negative—the financial transactions did not occur but otherwise would have. Second, the cyber conflict occurred during a military invasion, when additional and complicating factors affected overall economic performance. Third, any estimate of the damages resulting from the cyber attacks would require a joint effort by the government and private sector to estimate costs to private citizens, government security, and business services. It is likely that at least some of this information is either classified by the government or inaccessible due to laws designed to protect business confidentiality or personal privacy.[63]

In sum, there is no available data on the financial costs of the cyber attacks on Georgia. The attacks limited the government's ability to respond during a crisis and impaired a society's ability to gain information during an invasion and access financial services for ten days. The effects of the cyber attack lasted for more than a week, but ultimately did not cause permanent damage. Whatever the financial costs to Georgia were for this cyber attack, they were almost certainly more than the cost of the DDoS attack: according to Bill Woodcock, research director at the Packet Clearing House, a nonprofit organization that tracks internet traffic, it costs a mere 4 cents per machine for a DDoS attack.[64]

International Reaction

Russia

While the cyber attacks were under way, the Georgian Embassy in London accused Russia of launching the DoS attacks. A spokesperson for the embassy acknowledged that the attacks were still under investigation (indeed, still occurring in Georgia), but asked that given the circumstances of the ground invasion, "Who else might it be, though?" The Russian Embassy in London responded with a statement that it had no knowledge of the cyber attacks and insisted that there had been no military attacks against Georgia. It characterized the deployment of troops into Georgia as "peace enforcement in South Ossetia."[65]

Assigning blame and holding actors responsible for the cyber attacks requires knowing who was involved in the attacks. The Russian government denies responsibility for the cyber attacks against Georgia.[66] It is possible that a hacker group was responsible for the cyber attacks on Georgia. Some hacker organizations claim responsibility for attacks because they are a way of building prestige and enhancing their reputation in the hacker community. Yet in other cases, ownership or responsibility of the attack is never claimed and must be discerned from the forensic IT evidence, if possible. In the case of the cyber attacks on Georgia, no group claimed responsibility and the forensic IT evidence was not able to prove or disprove conclusively Russian government involvement in the attacks.[67]

As with Estonia, there is no conclusive proof of who is responsible for the cyber attacks. Project Grey Goose, one of the most comprehensive and widely cited investigations of the cyber attacks in Georgia, reports that the level of preparation and reconnaissance involved in the attacks strongly suggests that Russian hackers acted in consultation or coordination with Russian government or military officials.[68]

While IT experts admit that there is no definitive proof of Russian government involvement, there is some evidence of RBN involvement. Reports indicated that the RBN did not necessarily conduct the attacks directly but hosted the botnet command-and-control servers (bulletproof networks) that coordinated the attacks.[69] At least six different botnet command-and-control servers were involved with the attacks against government and nongovernment websites based in Georgia, according to the Shadowserver Foundation, an organization of security professionals who gather information on cybercrime.[70] According to experts, these botnet command-and-control servers are either "DDoS for hire" or "DDoS extortion" services, most of which have a known history of conducting attacks against commercial entities. It is rare, however, to see these servers being used in attacks against noncommercial (government) organizations.[71] It is these command-and-control servers that conducted the attacks on the websites, while the RBN was merely a hosting provider.[72]

A website called "The RBN Website," which normally tracks RBN activities online, closely monitored the cyber attacks on Georgia. According to its analysis, the Russian-based servers AS12389 Rostelecom, AS8342 Rtcomm, and AS8359 Comstar controlled all traffic to Georgia's key servers during the attacks. For a few hours on August 9, German hackers were able to reroute traffic through Deutsche Telekom's AS3320 DTAG server, but it was intercepted quickly and rerouted through the Moscow-based AS8359 Comstar.[73]

Despite the circumstantial evidence and implicit ties to Russia, forensic IT evidence and RBN involvement still does not prove or disprove the Russian government's involvement in the cyber attacks. Russian military cyber doctrine endorses cyber warfare, and statements by officials have been supportive of attacks conducted by hackers in the interest of the state, but there is no direct evidence that the Russian government orchestrated the attacks on Georgia.[74]

Circumstantial evidence does make it appear that Russia at least tolerated, if not directly supported, the cyber attacks in Georgia. The cyber attacks took place during a political dispute between Russia and Georgia. The cyber attacks coincided with the movement of Russian military forces across the border into South Ossetia. Coordination and instructions for the attacks took place on Russian-language internet forums and used RBN hosting services. According to Project Grey Goose, the cyber attacks on Georgia were likely to have been coordinated by some organization because they comprised five stages: encouraging activists to become involved in the cyber war against Georgia; publishing a list of accessible targets; selecting malware for use in the attacks; launching the cyber attacks; and evaluating the results.[75]

The internet trail of ownership and payment for the websites involved in the cyber attacks led to inconclusive results. The website StopGeorgia.ru led to a relatively anonymous Russian individual (who has a surprisingly small internet footprint) and a small company that is located, coincidentally, in an apartment building next to a Russian Ministry of Defense Research Institute called the Center for Research of Military Strength of Foreign Countries, which is situated down the road from the headquarters of the foreign military intelligence directorate of the General Staff of the Armed Forces (GRU). The GRU's mission is political and aimed at military information gathering in foreign countries. For this purpose, it deploys spies to foreign countries and leverages signal intelligence from electronic mediums and image intelligence from satellite imagery. The organization has also admitted that technical espionage, including hacking of computer networks to gain access to sensitive information, and open-source intelligence are among its missions.[76]

In 2008 after a thorough investigation, the highly reputable Project Grey Goose reported:

> We assess with high confidence that the Russian government will likely continue its practice of distancing itself from the Russian nationalistic hacker community thus gaining deniability while passively supporting and enjoying the strategic benefits of their actions.
>
> While forum members are quite open about their targets and methods, we were unable in this round of collection/analysis to find any references to state organizations guiding or directing attacks. There are several possible explanations as to why this is the case.
>
> - There was no external involvement or direction from State organizations.
> - Our collection efforts were not far-reaching or deep enough to identify these connections.
> - Involvement by State organizations was done in an entirely nonattributable way.[77]

One year later, speculation of Russian government involvement in the cyber attacks renewed when the Russian media reported that the Russian government pays youth groups to engage in information operations, including hacking into websites to silence dissident groups. The two main youth organizations accused of such activities are Nashi and United Russia. Nashi reportedly receives its funding from Russian businesses owners, but there is widespread speculation that it also receives government funding. One Nashi member has even admitted to being paid by the Kremlin in exchange for participating in opposition youth political movements.[78]

Despite the lack of proof of Russian government involvement, there is a strong argument to be made for larger Russian accountability in the cyber attacks. The Russian government collects and controls the data generated within its borders and is responsible for the activities of citizens or organizations acting within its territory. According to an interview with the editor-in-chief of Russian news site BFM.ru, the Russian government copies every byte of internet traffic from businesses and households within its borders and sends it to the Federal Security Service (FSB). Furthermore, the Russian government either owns the infrastructure of the internet within its borders or controls the licenses of all communications channels in Russia.[79] Thus, while the Russian government may not have been involved in the cyber attacks, it had the capability to end them—and it chose not to.

The EU and Its Member States

Georgia is not a member of the EU; its relationship is governed by the Partnership and Cooperation Agreement (PCA), signed in 1999. The PCA provides the legal framework for cooperation in trade, investment, political dialogue, and economic, legislative, and cultural matters. Georgia is also part of the EU's European Neighbor Policy (ENP). In 2006, the EU and Georgia signed an ENP five-year action plan geared toward improving economic cooperation and deepening political cooperation.[80]

The EU was not a formal party to conflict-resolution negotiations following the 2008 war between Russia and Georgia, but its member states played several roles.[81] French president Nicholas Sarkozy, the head of the EU presidency at the time, brokered a ceasefire between Russia and Georgia on August 12, 2008. The ceasefire agreement included a six-point plan that required both sides to agree to cessation of violence and free access for humanitarian aid, return to prewar positions, and engage in discussions on the future stability and security of Abkhazia and South Ossetia. Sarkozy initially refrained from criticizing Russia's use of disproportionate force, but that changed when Russia refused to withdraw troops to prewar positions and recognized the independence of Abkhazia and South Ossetia. At that point, Sarkozy requested an emergency summit of the European Commission (only the third in is history) to review EU relations with Russia.[82]

The EU held an emergency summit on September 1, 2008, during which it discussed possible sanctions against Russia, including tightening of the visa system. Ultimately, it decided to postpone renewal of the partnership pact with Moscow until Russian troops were withdrawn to their prewar positions. The EU also condemned Russia's recognition of the independence of South Ossetia and Abkhazia (which occurred on August 26, 2008)[83] and pledged to review its foreign relations with Russia.[84]

The crisis in Georgia exposed the limits of the EU's effectiveness in negotiating foreign policy matters. Despite agreeing to the six-point peace plan, Russia delayed the withdrawal of troops from Georgia and created new buffer zones inside Georgian territory. Furthermore, while EU states were united in their condemnation of Russia's recognition of Abkhazia and South Ossetia, they were divided in how to respond. The more recent EU member states, particularly the former Soviet states in Eastern Europe, argued for swift and strong response to Russian aggression, which they view as a major threat to European security. The more western EU states that had developed relatively good economic relations with Russia, such as Italy and Germany, sought a more nuanced approach and were more circumspect about criticizing Russian action. The lack of a unified position among the member states was exacerbated by the EU being highly dependent on Russian energy supplies: it receives approximately one-third of its oil and 40 percent of its natural gas from Russia.[85]

Despite the disunity on a policy toward Russia, the EU was united in providing support to Georgia. It provided crisis-response assistance to Georgia in the form of financial aid: five months after the conflict, the EU had provided €120 million in postcrisis assistance to Georgia, in addition to its €42 million of regular funding. The objective of the assistance was to provide humanitarian aid, support internally displaced persons, stabilize the security situation, repair infrastructure, and support the economic recovery of Georgia.[86] Individual EU member countries also provided €8.4 million in support.[87]

Poland, Ukraine, and the Baltic States

Poland and other Eastern European states stood by Georgia during the attacks. President Lech Kaczynski of Poland, President Toomas Hendrik Ilves of Estonia, President Valdis Zatlers of Latvia, President Valdas Adamkus of Lithuania, and President Viktor Yushchenko of Ukraine traveled to Tbilisi on August 12, 2008, to demonstrate their support of Georgia. A few days prior, the same presidents issued a joint statement urging the EU and NATO to "stand up against the spread of imperialist and revisionist policy" by Russia.[88] The presidents of the former Soviet states argued that NATO's refusal to fast-track Georgian membership into NATO was tantamount to giving Russia a "green light" for aggression, and the latest violence was Russia showing its "true face" once again.[89]

Poland in particular provided real-time assistance to Georgia during the cyber attacks. Upon request by the president of Georgia, Poland provided the president's website as a host site for dissemination of information about the attacks on Georgia. The Georgian government was able to use this site to communicate with the international community and any Georgians who had access to the internet. It was through this site that Georgia was able to accuse Russia of blocking Georgian internet portals to create a cyber blockade, bombing the port of Poti on the Black Sea (a vital energy-transit route to Europe), and sending warships into the area.[90]

Estonia also provided real-time assistance to Georgia during the crisis. Estonian president Ilves urged the EU to act strongly in the face of Russian incursions into Georgian territory and argued that both NATO and the EU should offer membership to Georgia and Ukraine in order to enable them to resist Russian interference and deter Russian aggression.[91] Furthermore, Estonia sent its CERT to Georgia to help defend against the DDoS attacks as they were in progress.

NATO

Georgia-NATO relations began in 1992, when a newly independent Georgia joined the North Atlantic Cooperation Council (which became the Euro-Atlantic Partnership Council in 1997). In 1994, Georgia joined the Partnership for Peace program, which was designed to assist European countries with the transitions required to achieve full NATO membership. Georgia's relationship with NATO continued to progress, and after the 2003 Rose Revolution, NATO increased its focus on supporting democratic reforms in Georgia.

At the time of the cyber attacks, Georgia was engaged in pursuing active political dialogue and practical cooperation with NATO as part of the Partnership for Peace program. Georgia was a NATO partner that actively participated in NATO missions such as the International Security Assistance Force (ISAF) in Afghanistan and Operation Active Endeavor in the Mediterranean,[92] but it was not yet a member of the alliance and, as such, could not invoke Article 5 for defense against an external threat.[93]

Despite US urging at the Bucharest Summit of April 2008, NATO decided not to offer a Membership Action Plan (MAP) to Georgia immediately, but agreed to review that decision in December 2008. (The MAP is the final step before NATO membership.) NATO secretary general Scheffer said in a news conference that Georgia would become a NATO member eventually, a decision that has since been reconfirmed in subsequent summits. Georgian diplomats were not happy about the delay, but were pleased with the promise of eventual membership.[94]

The delay in offering Georgia a MAP was reportedly due to German and French concerns about angering Russia. Russian foreign minister Sergei Lavrov had said that Russia would do everything in its power to prevent Ukraine and Georgia from joining NATO. From the Russian perspective, the extension of the alliance would pose a direct threat to its security and endanger the balance of power in Europe.[95] Russia's deputy foreign minister Alexander Grushko was quoted as saying, "Georgia's and Ukraine's membership in the alliance is a huge strategic mistake which would have most serious consequences for pan-European security."[96] Russian general Yuri Baluyevsky also went on record, ominously threatening that "Russia will take steps aimed at ensuring its interests along its borders . . . . These will not only be military steps, but also steps of a different nature."[97]

According to some experts, the Russian invasion of Georgia had little to do with Georgia and its separatist regions; rather, the conflict over the autonomous region was a pretext for deterring NATO expansion into Georgia and intimidating other potential NATO members. The disproportionate attacks on Georgia were a warning to other border states that might seek inclusion into the Western security umbrella. The message was that former Soviet states could not count on NATO to protect them from Russian aggression. The attacks could also be viewed as validation of the arguments put forth by European statesmen who argued for caution in extending NATO membership to Georgia; had Georgia been a member and requested assistance under Article 5, NATO would have been obligated to become involved in a war with Russia for the first time in the alliance's history.[98]

On August 12, NATO convened an extraordinary meeting of the allied ambassadors to discuss the events in Georgia, more than four days after the invasion began. On August 19, NATO held a special foreign ministerial session of the North Atlantic Council (NAC), which called for a peaceful resolution that respected Georgia's independence, territorial integrity, and sovereignty.[99] NATO expressed deep concern over the conflict and the disproportionate use of force by the Russian military, which was incompatible with its role as a peacekeeping force in South Ossetia and Abkhazia. NATO called on Russia to withdraw its military forces immediately and abide by the terms of agreement brokered by the EU in its six-point plan.[100] According to some scholars, given NATO's fourteen-year relationship with Georgia, the ministerial meeting was a weak signal of resolve, which may have led Russia to downplay the gravity of the message. A stronger signal of intent might have been to convene a meeting of the NAC at the highest level, if only to demonstrate the severity of the situation.[101]

NATO also provided assistance and support to Georgia and sent a team of experts to the country. In particular, it agreed to help assess the damage to civil infrastructure, the Ministry of Defense, and the armed forces, as well as support the reestablishment of the air traffic system and advise on cyber defense issues. On August 27, 2008, the NAC condemned Russia's decision to recognize the independence of South Ossetia and Abkhazia and called on Russia to reverse its decision.[102]

To assist with recovery efforts in Georgia after the war, NATO established the NATO-Georgia Commission in September 2008 as a consultative framework to oversee the implementation of support and recovery measures and assist with the development of an annual national program. NATO continues to recognize the territorial integrity and sovereignty of Georgia within its internationally recognized borders, which include South Ossetia and Abkhazia.[103]

At the first meeting of the NATO-Georgia Commission, NATO secretary general Scheffer criticized Russian violation of the EU's six-point peace plan, which included stationing 7,600 troops in Abkhazia and South Ossetia, twice the prewar level. Scheffer said, "I don't see this as a return to the status quo." The secretary general also criticized the peace plan for its vagueness and the EU for offering too many concessions to Russia and not opposing Russian violation of the agreement.[104]

A few months after the cyber attacks on Georgia, NATO released an extensive report called *Cyber Attacks against Georgia: Legal Lessons Identified*, which analyzed the cyber attacks and their international implications. It also compared the facts to the legal lessons identified in a similar report after the Estonia cyber attacks. The goal of the report was to discern trends in cyber attacks and identify their implications for the current international legal framework.[105]

United States

After the 2003 Rose Revolution, the United States invested heavily in Georgia's democratization because it saw the revolution as evidence of the theory that support for reformers and Western-oriented elites could promote favorable political change. In 2004, Georgia committed a large contingent of troops to the war in Iraq. A year later, President Bush visited Tbilisi to reinforce the strategic partnership between the countries and called Georgia a "beacon of democracy" in the region.[106]

The United States was one of Georgia's staunchest allies before the attacks. The United States stationed 130 military advisers plus civilian advisers and contractors in Georgia to assist the Georgian government, military, and businesses. According to some political analysts, the countries were so close that it is inconceivable that the United States did not know in advance about Georgia's plan to take South Ossetia by force. At the same time, if Russia knew of Georgia's plans (it appears it did, based on military preparations and prepositioning of forces), then it would be surprising if the United States did not know of Russia's troop posture, which would have been obvious because of its satellite imagery, signals intelligence, technical intelligence, and unmanned aerial systems.[107] Yet according to the secretary of Georgia's NAC during the war, Alexander Lomaia, "neither we nor any foreign intelligence service had any information about Russia's expected full-scale invasion and occupation of a large part of our territory—it was a shock and a surprise."[108]

When the attacks occurred, the United States condemned them and President Bush issued a statement criticizing Russia's "disproportionate" use of force. Vice President Dick Cheney also said that Russia's use of force in Georgia must not go unanswered and there would be serious consequences for Moscow's relationship with the West if the aggression persisted. The specific consequences were not spelled out, but Russian expulsion from the G-8 was widely considered to be one of them.[109]

Notably, the United States did not threaten the use of force in response to Russian aggression. The United States was engaged in two wars in the Middle East and its military was stretched thin by years of extended deployments. Regardless of the United States' political view of the crisis, it was simply not in a position to take any military action in defense of Georgia. Some analysts have argued that this was precisely the response that Russia anticipated and hoped for because American inaction sent the message that US security guarantees could not be relied upon when its forces are tied down in other regions. Thus, the invasion of Georgia could be interpreted as a warning for other states like Poland and the Czech Republic that chose to align themselves with the United States and against Russian interests, such as ballistic missile defense systems in Europe.[110]

Some US policymakers viewed the attacks on Georgia as an exemplary reason for Georgia's inclusion into NATO. If Georgia were a NATO member that could invoke Article 5 for self-defense, then Russia might not act as aggressively toward it. According to Senator John McCain, NATO's decision to delay a MAP to Georgia "might have been viewed as a green light by Russia for its attacks on Georgia," and he urged that NATO revisit its decision.[111]

The United States did not provide direct military support to Georgia during the crisis, although it had been involved in training and equipping the Georgian military for several years. Instead, the United States deployed several naval vessels with humanitarian supplies to the Black Sea to assist with the recovery and show solidarity with Tbilisi.[112]

Analysis

The facts and circumstances of the cyber attacks against Georgia in 2008 lend themselves to analysis according to the theory of cyber blockades presented earlier. As with the Estonian attacks, the primary issues for analysis are the actions undertaken, the actors involved, their capabilities, the preexistence of conflict, and the rights of neutrals. In addition, this section also analyzes the contributing factors that help identify the circumstances or conditions under which cyber blockades are likely to occur. These include the vulnerabilities, goals of the attack, and alternative courses of action.

Actions

The cyber attacks sought to cut off Georgia's access to cyberspace and its associated technologies in order to prevent the transmission of data and information beyond its borders. The timing of the attacks makes it likely that the cyber attackers specifically wanted to prevent the transmission of information about the Russian military invasion of Georgia and undermine the government's ability to function during an existential crisis.

Actors

The actors involved in the cyber attacks against Georgia were both state and nonstate actors. The state actor was the target, the Republic of Georgia. The government of Russia is widely suspected to have supported or coordinated the attacks, but its involvement has never been proven. The perpetrators of the cyber attacks were not caught, but most experts agree that the attacks were carried out by individuals and organizations, such as the RBN, that were sympathetic to the Russian political view of Georgia and South Ossetia. These nonstate actors allegedly created the malware, posted it to Web forums, protected the forums with "bullet-proof" servers, vetted and published information about the targets, rented and deployed botnets for DDoS, and downloaded malware from Web forums to launch DDoS attacks.

Since the perpetrators of the cyber attacks were not definitively identified, it is impossible to comment on their rationality with complete confidence. However, assuming that the attackers were the nonstate actors listed above, rationality can be inferred based on the circumstances. It is known that the attackers downloaded the malware from Russian-language sites and that the host sites and servers could be traced back to individuals and organizations in Russia. Some of these organizations, like the RBN, are criminal networks that operate within Russia with the complicity of the Russian government. Thus, it could be considered rational for these individuals or organizations to attack Georgian websites out of a sense of patriotic duty for Russia or as a result of prompting by the Russian government.

If the Russian government itself was involved in the cyber attacks, this too would be completely rational. Since Russia was already involved in a military confrontation with Georgia, it would be expected to use any of its relevant capabilities to win the war or achieve its objective. Also, if Russia urged nonstate actors to launch the cyber attacks, this would also be rational, since it gives Russia plausible deniability in the attacks but achieves the same ultimate objective.

Capabilities

The capabilities required to launch this attack included malware for DDoS attacks, host sites for the sharing of information, bullet-proof servers to keep IT experts from shutting down the attacks quickly, and access to botnet herds. The last of these can be rented from criminal elements on the black market, but it requires a significant amount of money to rent botnet herds for the length of time and level of intensity of the attacks in Georgia. Also, attackers need expertise in hacking and IT to create and distribute the malware in the first place.

The perpetrators of the cyber attacks on Georgia had some knowledge of the vulnerabilities of the Georgian websites and the impact DDoS attacks would have on the country. They also had the hacking expertise to conduct the attacks and the foresight to vet the targeted sites for access. In addition, it appears that they had prior knowledge of the Russian military involvement in South Ossetia and were prepared to act in conjunction with that assault in order to increase effectiveness (and possibly diminish the chances of being caught).

Preexistence of Conflict

The presence of ongoing hostilities or a "frozen conflict" is a contributing factor in the cyber attacks on Georgia. The perpetrators were acting in support of the Russian government (if not directly for it) when they launched the cyber attacks against Georgia. Presumably, these cyber attacks would not have occurred absent the political tension between Russia and Georgia that had been building for years, particularly in the months prior to the attacks.

The cyber attacks against Georgia took place in the context of a ground invasion and a shooting war between Russia and Georgia. The larger conflict itself is referred to as the Georgia-Russia War, thus it would seem appropriate that any attacks during that conflict—particularly those that targeted the Office of the President, the financial sector, and communications—would be considered part of the wartime effort. Nevertheless, had the cyber attacks occurred absent the military conflict, they might not have been declared acts of war or considered *casus belli* for war.

Rights of Neutrals

The cyber attacks on Georgia did not interfere with the rights of neutrals, except for those who happened to be in Georgia or seeking to exchange data or information with Georgia through cyberspace at the time of the attacks. The cyber attackers had the ability to target specific sectors and chose to target the Georgian government websites, communications information, and financial transactions. This hindered the government's operations, impaired its ability to communicate effectively during a major crisis, and weakened the Georgian economy—but did not interfere with the rights of neutrals. The attacks targeted key nodes of Georgian communication infrastructure, thereby affecting most of the population of Georgia.

The right of neutrals in the Georgia case is particularly interesting because when the cyber attacks began, the government of Georgia moved several critical internet assets to other countries, such as Poland, Estonia, and the United States. While Poland and Estonia gave permission for this relocation, Georgia never asked the United States' permission and, instead, worked directly through Tulip Systems, a private Web-hosting company based out of Atlanta, Georgia (US).[113]

Thus, a private company based in the United States, with no clear authority and no apparent US government approval, arranged to protect Georgian government internet assets by moving them to US territory. The United States was not a party to the Georgia-Russia War and would have been considered a neutral state, but Tulip Systems' independent actions jeopardized US neutrality in the conflict and risked expanding the attacks to include Georgian sites hosted in the United States.[114]

Vulnerabilities

There are particular vulnerabilities associated with the cyber attack on Georgia that may be considered contributing factors. First, geography matters in this conflict. Georgia is located on Russia's southern flank and is therefore within Russia's perceived area of influence. Thus, Russia is interested in activities in Georgia because they may threaten its security, regional influence, or perception of prestige. Second, Georgia had relatively few internet servers that did not transit through Russia somewhere, and most Georgian internet traffic passed through Russia at some point. This feature allowed Russia (or Russian-speaking cyber attackers) greater access to and familiarity with the technological infrastructure on which Georgia depended. Third, Georgia has a relatively low dependency on IT services and capabilities. While this may seem to make it a less attractive target for cyber attacks, this may not be the case. Because it has relatively low dependency (especially compared with a country like Estonia), it had not created redundancies to make the system more resilient in the event of an attack. Countries that are highly technologically dependent tend to be more aware of their vulnerabilities and the potential problems that could arise as a result of these dependencies, thus they are more likely to invest in robust, redundant, and resilient systems. In the case of Georgia, redundancy was particularly important because it had a limited number of servers.

In contrast, Russia would be less likely to face the same issues with its IT infrastructure because its vast geography necessitates more options for servers and infrastructure. Because it is more dependent on IT, it may have a more highly developed IT sector, which is likely to include defensive measures, redundant capabilities, and resilient systems. Furthermore, the Russian government has developed strategies for information and cyber warfare, which indicates that it perceives cyber attacks as a threat and has probably already taken action to reduce its vulnerabilities.

Goals of the Cyber Attack

Without definitive attribution or claims of responsibility, the intended goals or consequence of the cyber attack can only be inferred from the information available. Because of the timing of the cyber attacks to coincide with a ground assault, it appears likely that a goal of the cyber attack was to deny the government of Georgia access to information in order to weaken its war efforts by limiting its capability and capacity for sustained warfare. It is not known if the Georgian military's command-and-control was affected by the cyber attack, but it is possible.

The cyber attacks on Georgia appeared to have several goals for the state and society. First, the cyber attacks isolated Georgia by limiting its access to information and interactions with foreign actors during a national crisis. This isolation limited the international political support and advice that Georgia could receive during an existential crisis. Second, the blockade placed financial constraints on Georgia by adversely affecting its ability to conduct financial transactions. The cyber attacks forced a cessation of electronic financial transactions for ten days.

Third, the cyber attacks placed pressure on the government and entire society, possibly as a method of rendering a psychological effect that would make Georgia more likely to comply with Russia's wishes. The cyber attacks lasted for only for a few weeks, but it was long enough to demonstrate the attackers' capability to control Georgia's access to cyberspace and use this control as an implicit threat for the future. In this respect, the demonstration of cyber capabilities is akin to the Russian military's repeated bombings around the Georgian oil pipeline; Russia demonstrated its ability to hold at risk and destroy the pipeline, if it so chose.

Alternative Courses of Action

In this particular case, it is unclear what the alternative courses of action may have been for nonstate actors. Cyberspace gives unprecedented and unparalleled power to nonstate actors to engage in international relations. The technology of this domain allows nonstate actors to have a disproportionate influence on events and eschew traditional diplomatic, economic, or military alternatives. The nature of technology in cyberspace also allows nonstate actors to preserve their anonymity, which may be desired if their actions are of questionable legality.

If Russia was truly behind the cyber attacks on Georgia, then the traditional alternative courses of action (diplomatic, economic, and military) are clear. In this particular case, Russia had already employed diplomatic and economic tools and progressed to military action against Georgia. In this context, a cyber attack would simply be a continuation of politics by other means.

Conclusion

The cyber attacks on Georgia in 2008 are an important case of cyber blockade because, like many other blockades through history, they occurred during the context of warfare. The cyber attacks were part of an organized military effort to harm Georgia, undermine the government, and destabilize the state. As such, it was one of several capabilities employed for these ends during the war.

The cyber attacks on Georgia fit all of the criteria for a blockade in cyberspace. The actions, actors, capability, preexistence of conflict, and rights of neutrals fit the theory, as do the contributing factors of specific vulnerabilities, goals of the blockade, and alternative courses of action.

The cyber blockade of Georgia varies from historical blockades in anticipated ways. The unique characteristics of the domain influenced the types of resources required for the cyber blockade, the vulnerabilities exploited, and the effects that the blockade had on the government and society. These variations based on the nature of the domain are expected of blockades in cyberspace, as well as in other domains.

There are several unique aspects of the cyber blockade of Georgia that are particular to the characteristics of the domain. Plausible deniability or the attackers' anonymity is possible only because of the attributes of cyberspace; in any other domain, it is more than likely that the blockading actor would be known to all. The cost of the cyber blockade was relatively low; botnets cost approximately 4 cents per machine for a botnet attack. The political costs of a cyber blockade would be higher, if only the attackers were known. Finally, the attack occurred rapidly: it began with the military invasion and ended a few weeks later. Given the timing and coordination required for the attack, it is likely that the perpetrators spent weeks or months preparing for the cyber blockade of Georgia but that

Russia spent even longer preparing its forces for the military invasion of Georgia.

Notes

1. Hollis, "Cyberwar Case Study: Georgia 2008," 2.

2. Markoff, "Before the Gunfire, Cyberattacks."

3. Tikk et al., "Cyber Attacks against Georgia: Legal Lessons Identified," 5–6; International Telecommunications Union, "Percentage of Individuals Using the Internet 2000–2010."

4. Zmijewski, "Georgia Clings to the 'Net,'"; Tikk et al., "Cyber Attacks against Georgia: Legal Lessons Identified," 8.

5. Tikk et al., "Cyber Attacks against Georgia: Legal Lessons Identified," 6.

6. Ukrainian News Agency, "Georgia Interested in Using Poti-Varna Fiber-Optic Cable for Joint Telecommunications Projects with Ukraine."

7. Golz, "The Paradox of Living in Paradise: Georgia's Descent into Chaos."

8. Slider, "Democratization in Georgia."

9. Golz, "The Paradox of Living in Paradise: Georgia's Descent into Chaos," 18.

10. Hollis, "Cyberwar Case Study: Georgia 2008."

11. Tikk et al., "Cyber Attacks against Georgia: Legal Lessons Identified," 4, 32.

12. Golz, "The Paradox of Living in Paradise: Georgia's Descent into Chaos," 18.

13. Tikk et al., "Cyber Attacks against Georgia: Legal Lessons Identified," 32–33.

14. Nilsson, "Georgia's Rose Revolution: The Break with the Past," 99–101.

15. Zarakhovich, "Will Russia Block Kosovo Independence?"

16. Finn, "Russia's Moves Add to Strains with Georgia."

17. BBC News, "Russia Army Unit Sent to Abkhazia."

18. Kurtbag, "E.U.'s Response to the Georgian Crisis: An Active Peace Broker or a Confused and Divided Actor?," 10.

19. Adair, "The Website for the President of Georgia under Attack—Politically Motivated?"

20. Markoff, "Before the Gunfire, Cyberattacks."

21. Felgenhauer, "After August 7: The Escalation of the Russia-Georgia War," 163–64.

22. These interviews and reports were published in different Russian newspapers and the official Defense Ministry daily *Krasnaya Zvezda* (Red Star). For more information, see ibid., 169.

23. Friedman, "The Russo-Georgian War and the Balance of Power."

24. Ibid.

25. Felgenhauer, "After August 7: The Escalation of the Russia-Georgia War," 163–65.

26. Sherr, "The Implications of the Russia-Georgia War for European Security," 212.

27. Part of the Russian message was that Saakashvili was the aggressor, thus he brought this war upon himself. For more information, see Felgenhauer, "After August 7: The Escalation of the Russia-Georgia War," 179, 83–92.

28. Hollis, "Cyberwar Case Study: Georgia 2008."

29. Goble, "Defining Victory and Defeat: The Information War between Russia and Georgia," 181.

30. Ibid., 182.

31. Tikk et al., "Cyber Attacks against Georgia: Legal Lessons Identified," 7.

32. Adair, "Georgian Websites under Attack—DDoS and Defacement."

33. Nazario, "Georgia DDoS Attacks—A Quick Summary of Observations."

34. Oltsik, "Russian Cyber Attack on Georgia: Lessons Learned?"

35. Tikk et al., "Cyber Attacks against Georgia: Legal Lessons Identified," 8.

36. Ibid.

37. Ibid., 8–9.

38. Ibid., 10.

39. "Сайты Риа Новости Подвергаются Непрерывным Dos-Атакам" [Websites of Ria Novosti are under continuous DoS attacks].

40. Zmijewski, "Georgia Clings to the 'Net."

41. TCP SYN stands for "transmission control protocol, synchronize message," which is the foundation for every connection made with TCP. TCP is one of the core protocols of the internet protocol suite (IP).

42. Nazario, "Georgia DDoS Attacks—A Quick Summary of Observations"; Carr, *Inside Cyber Warfare*, 83.

43. Tikk et al., "Cyber Attacks against Georgia: Legal Lessons Identified," 9.

44. The "cyber kill chain" has five steps: encourage novices to participate in cyber attacks; publish a vetted list of target sites; discuss and select several types of malware to use against the targets; launch the attacks; and discuss results. For more information, see Carr et al., "Project Grey Goose: Phase I Report: Russia/Georgia Cyber War—Findings and Analysis."

45. Krebs, "Report: Russian Hacker Forums Fueled Georgia Cyber Attacks."

46. The Russian Business Network rose to prominence and began earning high profits in 2007 by selling "bulletproof networks." Bulletproof networks are defined as "a series of business relationships that make it extremely difficult for authorities to shut down web enterprises engaged in criminal activities," according to Carr, *Inside Cyber Warfare*, 105. See also Krebs, "Report: Russian Hacker Forums Fueled Georgia Cyber Attacks"; Carr et al., "Project Grey Goose Phase II Report: The Evolving State of Cyber Warfare," 15.

47. Krebs, "Report: Russian Hacker Forums Fueled Georgia Cyber Attacks."

48. Carr et al., "Project Grey Goose: Phase I Report: Russia/Georgia Cyber War—Findings and Analysis," 9–10.

49. Krebs, "Report: Russian Hacker Forums Fueled Georgia Cyber Attacks."

50. Tikk et al., "Cyber Attacks against Georgia: Legal Lessons Identified," 10–11.

51. "Russian Invasion of Georgia: Russian Cyberwar on Georgia," 5.

52. Ibid. This was an anonymous report that is favorable to Georgia and is posted on a website owned by the government of Georgia, so the reliability of the report has not been determined. See Tikk et al., "Cyber Attacks against Georgia: Legal Lessons Identified," 11; also, www.georgiaupdate.gove.ge for more information about the site.

53. "Информационная Блокада" [Information blockade].

54. "Hacked by: Матричные Войны" [Hacked by: Matrix Wars].

55. Ibid.

56. "У Здания Грузинского Посольства В Москве Разбит Палаточный Городок" [A tent camp in front of the building of the Georgian embassy]; "На Сайте Мид Грузии

Появился Коллаж С Гитлером" [A photo collage with Hitler appeared on the webpage of the Georgian Foreign Ministry].

57. Normally the Georgian CERT provides computer and network security support for the Georgian institutions of higher education.

58. Tikk et al., "Cyber Attacks against Georgia: Legal Lessons Identified," 15.

59. Goble, "Defining Victory and Defeat: The Information War between Russia and Georgia," 191.

60. Tikk et al., "Cyber Attacks against Georgia: Legal Lessons Identified," 15–16.

61. Ibid., 16.

62. Ibid.

63. Ibid.

64. Markoff, "Before the Gunfire, Cyberattacks."

65. Espiner, "Georgia Accuses Russia of Coordinated Cyberattack."

66. Markoff, "Before the Gunfire, Cyberattacks."

67. Carr et al., "Project Grey Goose Phase II Report: The Evolving State of Cyber Warfare."

68. Krebs, "Report: Russian Hacker Forums Fueled Georgia Cyber Attacks."

69. Tikk et al., "Cyber Attacks against Georgia: Legal Lessons Identified," 12.

70. Adair, "Georgian Websites under Attack—DDoS and Defacement."

71. Past targets of these botnet command-and-control servers include websites engaged in promoting or organizing prostitution, adult videos, online gaming, white supremacy, trade in stolen credit cards, and certain news organizations.

72. Johnson, "Georgian Websites under Attack—Don't Believe the Hype."

73. Espiner, "Georgia Accuses Russia of Coordinated Cyberattack."

74. Tikk et al., "Cyber Attacks against Georgia: Legal Lessons Identified," 13.

75. Ibid., 13–14.

76. Carr et al., "Project Grey Goose Phase II Report: The Evolving State of Cyber Warfare," 17–20.

77. Ibid., 20.

78. Ibid., 21.

79. Ibid., 23.

80. European Union, "Summary on EU-Georgia Relations."

81. Ibid.

82. Kurtbag, "E.U.'s Response to the Georgian Crisis: An Active Peace Broker or a Confused and Divided Actor?," 61.

83. Levy, "Russia Backs Independence of Georgian Enclaves."

84. European Union, "Summary on EU-Georgia Relations"; Kurtbag, "E.U.'s Response to the Georgian Crisis: An Active Peace Broker or a Confused and Divided Actor?"

85. Kurtbag, "E.U.'s Response to the Georgian Crisis: An Active Peace Broker or a Confused and Divided Actor?," 62–63.

86. *Europa*, "European Commission's Crisis Response Assistance to Georgia in 2008 Reaches 120 Million."

87. European Union, "Summary on EU-Georgia Relations."

88. Bennhold, "Differences Emerge in Europe of a Response to Georgia Conflict."

89. Ibid.

90. Espiner, "Georgia Accuses Russia of Coordinated Cyberattack."

91. Feifer, "Estonia Seeks Stronger E.U. Response to Russia."

92. ISAF-Afghanistan is the stability and reconstruction effort in Afghanistan. Operation Active Endeavor is a counterterrorism maritime surveillance operation in the Mediterranean Sea.

93. North Atlantic Treaty Organization, "NATO's Relations with Georgia."

94. BBC News, "NATO Denies Georgia and Ukraine."

95. Shchedrov and Lowe, "Russia Army Vows Steps If Georgia and Ukraine Join Nato."

96. BBC News, "NATO Denies Georgia and Ukraine."

97. Shchedrov and Lowe, "Russia Army Vows Steps if Georgia and Ukraine Join NATO."

98. Karon, "The Georgia Crisis: A Blow to NATO."

99. Sherr, "The Implications of the Russia-Georgia War for European Security," 209.

100. North Atlantic Treaty Organization, "NATO's Relations with Georgia"; North Atlantic Treaty Organization, "NATO's Foreign Ministers Reiterate Their Support for Georgia."

101. Sherr, "The Implications of the Russia-Georgia War for European Security," 209–10.

102. North Atlantic Treaty Organization, "NATO's Relations with Georgia."

103. Ibid.

104. Kurtbag, "E.U.'s Response to the Georgian Crisis: An Active Peace Broker or a Confused and Divided Actor?," 69–70.

105. Tikk et al., "Cyber Attacks against Georgia: Legal Lessons Identified."

106. Nilsson, "Georgia's Rose Revolution: The Break with the Past," 99.

107. Friedman, "The Russo-Georgian War and the Balance of Power."

108. Felgenhauer, "After August 7: The Escalation of the Russia-Georgia War," 163.

109. Womack, "Nato Joins U.S. in Condemning Russia's Response in South Ossetia."

110. Friedman, "The Russo-Georgian War and the Balance of Power."

111. Karon, "The Georgia Crisis: A Blow to Nato."

112. Kurtbag, "E.U.'s Response to the Georgian Crisis: An Active Peace Broker or a Confused and Divided Actor?," 59.

113. Korns and Kastenberg, "Georgia's Cyber Left Hook."

114. Ibid., 67.

CHAPTER 6

Comparing Cyber Blockades

"Technology has been the handmaiden of change, and, especially recently, it has had to bear the burden of making blockades operationally effective. Blockade law has not evolved to meet the new demands placed upon it."

—Roger Barnett in "Technology and Naval Blockade"

Introduction

The preceding chapters presented a preliminary theory of blockades in cyberspace and examined the cyber attacks on Estonia in 2007 and Georgia in 2008 in light of that preliminary theory. The goals of this chapter are twofold. The first goal is to compare the cases of Estonia and Georgia to see how they differ. To this end, this chapter presents a comparative analysis of the cyber attacks on Estonia and Georgia in order to identify their similarities and differences. The second goal is to answer the questions proposed at the beginning of this research, specifically: What are cyber blockades and how do they compare with other types of blockades? And why do actors use cyber blockades as tools of international relations? To answer those questions, this chapter also compares these cases of cyber blockades to the previous analysis of blockades in other domains.

The answers to these questions are revealed through a comparative analysis using the framework presented in Chapter 3. The analysis examines the defining characteristics of blockade operations (e.g., actions, actors, capabilities, preexistence of conflict, and the rights of neutrals) and the

< 128 >

contributing factors to blockades (e.g., the vulnerabilities, results of blockade, and alternative courses of action). This chapter also draws lessons from these analyses for the implications of how the technology of cyberspace creates new capabilities within that domain that affect the historical understanding of blockade operations.

What Are Cyber Blockades, and How Do They Compare with Other Types of Blockades?

Chapter 3 sets forth five requirements in the preliminary theory of blockades. This section examines each of these requirements in the cases of Estonia and Georgia and compares the similarities and differences between them.

Actions

The cyber attacks in both Georgia and Estonia severed the countries' access to cyberspace and its associated technologies for a specific period of time. The attacks prevented the transmission or exchange of information or data through cyberspace from or within the targeted country. In both cases, the cyber attacks appeared to be part of an organized political campaign to undermine the credibility of the government of the targeted state.

Actors

In the case of Estonia, only one individual, Dmitri Galushkevich, was ever held accountable for the cyber attacks of 2007. Under existing laws, he was fined for participating in the cyber attacks. (Estonian laws have since been updated to address the growing threat and severity of cyber attacks directed against the state.) There was no evidence that Galushkevich acted on behalf of an organization or government, but it is widely suspected that Russia was involved, directly or indirectly, in the cyber attacks. Despite the suspicion of Russian involvement, there is no evidence to directly link Russia to the attacks.

In the case of Georgia, the perpetrators were never identified or caught. It is likely that the cyber attacks were conducted by individuals who may or may not have been acting with the support or encouragement of Russia. The Russian government is suspected of being involved in orchestrating,

directing, or at least tolerating the cyber attacks that appear to have originated from within the country's borders.

In both cases, the target of the cyber attacks was an internationally recognized, sovereign, territorial state. Both countries are former Soviet states
that share a border with Russia. Both are members of the international community and participate in European social, political, economic, and defense
activities.

The perpetrators of both attacks are believed to be nonstate actors. In both
cases, the attackers accessed malware posted on Russian-language forums
and used it to conduct the attacks. Botnet herds were involved in both attacks,
making it likely that criminal organizations were somehow involved (or
hired) in the attacks and that many of the direct attacks came from zombie
computers used without the knowledge or consent of their owners.

In both cases, Russian involvement appeared likely, although forensic IT
evidence could not definitively prove this. Russian political, economic, and
military activities at the time of the cyber attacks, including threats, sanctions,
and military invasion, cast a long shadow of suspicion on that country. These
circumstances, combined with Russian military doctrine for cyber warfare,
the likely involvement of the Russian Business Network (RBN), the involvement of computers within Russia, and the Russian refusal to cooperate with
investigations into the cyber attacks, make it difficult to believe that Russia
was not involved in the cyber attacks, either directly or indirectly. Nevertheless, the presence of nonstate actors (albeit Russian-speaking individuals)
provides plausible deniability for the government of Russia.

All of the actors involved in the cyber attacks on Estonia and Georgia
can be considered rational. Estonia and Georgia, the victims, were certainly
rational actors that responded to threats to their communications and information infrastructure and technology. Both reacted in appropriate ways
that demonstrated a range of political resources and technical capabilities
and were consistent with international laws and treaties.

If it is assumed that the nonstate actors acted in accordance with political
beliefs such as nationalistic pride for Russia or ethical reasons such as the
objection to the relocation of a gravesite, then their actions appear rational,
although not legal. The evidence of both circumstances suggests that the
nonstate actors believed they were helping to support a specific cause and
bring justice to a state that was acting in such a way as to threaten the
belief system endorsed by the nonstate actors. If the nonstate actors were
supported or encouraged by Russia, then they were also acting in support
of their ethnic, linguistic, or national homeland.

Assuming Russian involvement, it is also a rational and calculating actor displaying a range of capabilities that implicitly threaten other states while simultaneously avoiding direct confrontation. Russian involvement in the attacks would mean that it used proxy cyber forces to conduct attacks against another state while gaining plausible deniability. Russia maintains its position that it was not involved in either cyber attack, yet it would be rational for Russia to use nonstate actors or proxy groups to conduct attacks on its behalf, thereby achieving the objective of threatening or weakening the target state while preserving Russia's status and credibility in the international community.

Capabilities

The cyber attacks on Estonia and Georgia were very similar—both employed distributed denial-of-service (DDoS) attacks to disrupt traffic to and from specific sites for an extended period of time. The capabilities required to conduct the attacks were also similar, although the Georgia attack demonstrated a greater level of sophistication, planning, and coordination. The main capabilities required to launch both DDoS attacks included the IT expertise to create the malware that launched the attacks; access to servers and forums to distribute information about the attacks, recruit attackers, and post the malware; access to botnet herds for hire; and the financial resources to hire sizable botnet herds for sustained attacks over days and weeks. In the case of Georgia, the attackers also employed "bullet-proof" servers to make it more difficult to track and remove information about the attacks, and the cyber attacks appeared to be coordinated with ground, air, and naval assaults.

Knowledge of the cyber landscape and vulnerabilities was important in Estonia and Georgia. In both cases, the perpetrators of the cyber attacks needed to understand the specific vulnerabilities of the IT sectors in each country and the potential impact of a cyber attack, particularly on the vetted sites in Georgia. In addition, the perpetrators needed the technical expertise to create the malware and distribute it anonymously.

Preexistence of Conflict

The theory of cyber blockade suggests that blockades must take place in the context of an extant conflict. Historically, these conflicts were marked by declarations of war, commencement of hostilities, armed conflict, or UN declarations. Formal declarations of war did not precede the cyber attacks in Estonia or Georgia, but the attacks did occur during conflicts.

In the case of Estonia, the cyber attacks occurred within the context of a political conflict. The dispute over the Bronze Monument began as a domestic dispute but took on international dimensions when Russia began issuing statements and threats regarding the plans to move the monument. At the time the cyber attacks commenced, there was an ongoing political dispute between Estonia and Russia. After the cyber attacks began, the conflict widened to include other diplomatic and economic measures.

In the case of Georgia, the preexisting conflict was the frozen conflict over the independence of South Ossetia and Abkhazia. Political disagreements, threats, military engagement (the downing of a Georgian unmanned aerial vehicle), and mobilization of forces near the border occurred in the weeks and months directly preceding the cyber attacks. The cyber attacks coincided with the invasion of Russian forces into South Ossetia and the commencement of a ground, air, and sea assault on Georgian territory.

Thus, Estonia and Georgia experienced massive cyber attacks in the context of an extant conflict. For both countries, the conflict was a political issue prior to the cyber attacks and escalated to economic or military actions once the attacks commenced. For Georgia, the escalation occurred rapidly because there was a history of violent conflict and warfare with Russia over the status of the autonomous regions.

Neither cyber attack was officially considered an act of war. The decision not to consider these activities acts of war may reflect the lack of development of international laws and norms regulating the use of cyberspace and the definition of cyber warfare and armed conflict in cyberspace. These decisions may change with the evolution of thought about cyber warfare in the future. The case of Estonia was a proving ground for the first cyber attack on a state, and the international community (NATO, in particular) did not have a framework for dealing with that type of attack. In the attacks on Georgia, it was less important to determine if the cyber attacks alone constituted acts of war because a) Georgia was already involved in a war with Russia and b) Georgia was not a member of NATO, so there was no option for it to widen the dispute by invoking Article 5. Thus, while neither cyber attack was officially considered an act of war, the circumstances of each suggest that they may not be appropriate cases for establishing precedent for determining cyber attacks as acts of war.

Rights of Neutrals

In the cases of Estonia and Georgia, the cyber attacks targeted a state, or specific sectors within the state, and did not violate the rights of neutrals to use cyberspace or its associated technologies. Neutrals may have been affected in their ability to transmit data or information with actors inside of the targeted state or to access information hosted on a site that was the subject of attack as a side effect, but in neither case were neutrals targeted for attack. Thus, neutrality and impartiality were preserved and neutrals continued to have the ability to use the rest of the domain relatively unimpeded and unaffected by the cyber blockades against Estonia and Georgia.

Why Do Actors Use Cyber Blockades as a Tool of International Relations?

Chapter 3 identified three contributing factors for blockades: vulnerabilities, results of blockades, and alternative courses of action. Each of the two cases had different contributing factors and circumstances, but the similarities and differences between them can help identify strengths and weaknesses in the proposed theory.

Vulnerabilities

Chapter 3 outlined three types of vulnerabilities as contributing factors for blockades. These vulnerabilities are geography, reliance on trade, and interconnectedness and access to international partners or markets. These vulnerabilities continue to be relevant for blockades or attacks in cyberspace.

In the case of Estonia, it was vulnerable to a cyber attack because it was highly dependent on technology, yet its system had technological weaknesses and vulnerabilities that could be exploited. Estonia's dependency on cyberspace made it more interconnected and granted greater access to international partners and markets than may have otherwise been the case. As a result, a successful cyber attack on Estonia degraded Estonia's actual capabilities and brought prestige for the belligerent.

In the case of Georgia, geography is a contributing factor because most of Georgia's internet infrastructure passed through Russia at some point, thus giving Russia direct access to Georgia's cyber lines of communication.

Georgia did not enjoy the same levels of interconnectedness or widespread access to international partners (as measured by internet penetration) as Estonia. However, this may have made the cyber attacks more devastating in Georgia because its system did not have some of the technological features of a more robust system with more advanced defenses or greater resiliency. Also, as a small state that was not part of the EU or NATO, Georgia did not have the political capital or military capabilities required for self-defense against the Russian military. Georgia depended on support from the international community to condemn Russian action and negotiate a peaceful settlement, thus Georgia was more vulnerable to cyber attacks that would impair its ability to gather international support.

Both Estonia and Georgia border Russia, the suspected aggressor in the cyber attacks, but only in the case of Georgia did geography make a difference in vulnerabilities. Geography and the Russian sphere of influence mattered greatly in the context for the conflicts, but direct access to cyber lines of communication was most important in the Georgia case. Reliance on trade seems of minimal importance in the cyber attacks on both countries. Interconnectedness and access to international partners made Estonia a more attractive target because by degrading Estonian capabilities, the aggressors gained prestige. Georgia's relatively limited interconnectedness meant that it was more vulnerable to attack because its IT system was less robust and cyber attacks could have greater consequences, compared with Estonia, which was able to mitigate the effects of the attack and return to normal activity quicker.

Goals of Blockade

The preliminary theory outlines four different goals of blockades: deny access to goods and information to weaken the adversary; deny access to specific goods to adversely affect the adversary's balance of trade; isolate an adversary by denying access to information or relationships with other actors in order to place pressure on the adversary; and create discomfort or suffering for the whole society, in the hopes that the government would capitulate to demands. While the specific goals of the perpetrators of the cyber attacks remain unknown, some of these goals appear applicable.

In the case of Estonia, there were three intended consequences of the cyber attacks. First, a goal was to create psychological distress by sowing disorder and fear during a time of political and social unrest. Second, the attacks appeared to seek to limit the government's capacity in retaliation for its political decision to move the monument. Third, the attacks may have been intended to bring down the main financial institutions in Estonia.

In Georgia, four potential goals of the cyber attacks can be identified. First, one goal was to deny the government the ability to access information and limit its command-and-control capabilities during a crisis. Second, the attacks also created disorder and fear within society at a time of acute crisis, creating psychological pressures on society and government. Third, the attacks isolated Georgia by limiting its access to support from the international community. Fourth, the attacks intended to undermine and harm the financial sector of Georgia.

In both cases, the attacks placed pressure on society and the government through the psychological distress caused by the disorder and fear of the cyber attacks. The attacks also sought to limit the state's national capacity to act, undermining the government's credibility. Third, both attacks targeted financial institutions, suggesting that the attackers may have intended to cause substantial financial damage, or at least indicate that it was possible, if the government did not change its course of action.

Alternative Courses of Action

When determining their courses of action, actors usually have many options. Alternatives for blockades may include diplomatic, economic, or military activities that may help them achieve the goals of isolating a geographic area and preventing the ingress and egress of goods and information. In Estonia and Georgia, several courses of action were employed in conjunction with the cyber attacks, but none was able to achieve the same result.

In Estonia, the nonstate actors had few options, which mainly consisted of political protest and perhaps legal measures challenging the government's decision. These options would not have rendered the same effect on the government, media, and financial sectors as the cyber attacks did. Russia also employed diplomatic and economic measures to isolate Estonia. In diplomacy, it called for the Estonian government to resign, signaling that it believed there was a reason to lack confidence in that government. In economic matters, it placed sanctions on Estonia and prevented the passage of goods via road and rail between the two countries.

In Georgia, nonstate actors may not have had many alternatives, aside from directly engaging in the military conflict. Russia used political tools and military action against Georgia, including reclaiming South Ossetia, threatening Tbilisi, and establishing an undeclared naval blockade on the Black Sea and an aerial blockade over much of Georgia in order to prevent the replenishment of supplies to that country. Thus, Russia appeared to use whatever means were at its disposal to weaken the state and prevent the ingress and egress of goods and information from Georgia.

While the actors in both the Georgia and Estonia cases employed alternative courses of action to undermine the governments and prevent the passage of goods and information in and out of the country, none of these actions could achieve the same results as cyber attacks. The political, economic, and military actions did not replace cyber attacks, but rather it appeared that the cyber attacks augmented these actions in order to increase effectiveness and create more harm (or the perception of the ability to create more harm).

Table 6.1 compares the cyber attacks on Estonia and Georgia based on the independent variables of targets, costs/resources, anonymity, legal status, and vulnerabilities that were presented in Chapter 1.

Table 6.1   Comparison of Estonia and Georgia Cases

	Estonia	**Georgia**
Targets	Government websites and functions Financial sector and transactions Media/communications organizations	Government websites Financial sector and transactions Media/communications organizations
Costs/Resources	Hardware (computers) Software (code) Expertise for launching attacks	Hardware (computers) Software (code) Expertise for launching attacks
Anonymity	Perpetrator not known	Perpetrator not known
Legal status	Not recognized as an act of war by international community	Not specifically recognized as an act of war by international community; part of larger context of war
Vulnerabilities	High level of dependence on cyber technologies Physical proximity to suspected aggressor	Low level of dependence on cyber technologies, but limited defenses and redundancies Physical proximity to suspected aggressor

How Do Cyber Blockades Compare with Blockades in Other Domains?

After examining the literature, the evolution of blockades in different domains, and the case studies of Estonia and Georgia, it is helpful to return to the original questions and hypotheses posited at the beginning of this research and see how they fare in light of the research. The main research questions sought to examine cyber blockades in general; the case studies of Estonia and Georgia were useful examples to illuminate the important aspects of blockades in cyberspace. This section consolidates what has been learned about cyber blockades and compares cyber blockades with blockades in other domains.

Cyber blockades are similar to blockades in other domains in several important aspects. The most important similarities of cyber and traditional blockades are their goals and approach. In cyberspace, land, air, sea, or space, the purpose of a blockade is to prevent the ingress and egress of data traffic and information to and from a territorial entity by degrading or denying its ability to access a specific domain. Naval, aerial, and land blockades focus on denying the passage of goods to the global market, but in an information economy the ability to use space or cyberspace to deny the passage of information to the global commons is equally important.

Blockades in cyberspace or elsewhere take place in the context of extant conflicts. Cyber blockades are tied to political relationships between and among international actors; they do not occur spontaneously or in a vacuum. In this respect, cyber blockades are similar to traditional blockades that are also instruments of force used to achieve political ends.

Traditional and cyber blockades both tend to target states or sovereign territorial entities, as opposed to individuals, nonstate actors, or multinational corporations. The perpetrators may come from any level of analysis, but the targets are territorial entities responsible for ensuring the safety and security of its citizens.

Despite implementing different measures and achieving different immediate results, cyber blockades and traditional blockades have similar effects on society. In both cases, society is denied access to goods and information that it normally accesses. This imposed denial of access reduces economic productivity and engenders frustration and uncertainty in society, since it is usually not known how long the denial will last and how routine business will be interrupted. This uncertainty creates fear and psychological distress in society, particularly if the cyber blockade occurs during a crisis that makes access to the information more important. Thus, the interruption of routine transactions for an unknown period of time occurs in both traditional and cyber blockades, creating fear and uncertainty in society.

Traditional and cyber blockades can target specific sectors such as government, financial, and communications sectors. Cyber blockades have the ability to be more precise in targeting within sectors (certain communications and media organizations, for example), but both types can target the goods and information produced within the target state. This ability to target the blockade, whether for specific types of steel, cotton, or information, is similar across all types of blockades.

How Does the Technology of Cyberspace Affect Our Understanding of Blockade Operations?

The previous section focused on how cyber blockades are similar to traditional blockades, but it is equally important to note the substantial ways in which cyber blockades differ from traditional blockades. The technology of cyberspace has created an environment in which different capabilities and effects are possible. This research is part of a broader effort to understand the ways in which technological change impacts social and political institutions within states, as well as interactions between and among different levels of analysis.

Cyber blockades differ from traditional blockades in several important ways. The actors in cyber blockades can be state or nonstate actors, including individuals, criminal organizations, or multinational organizations. In particular, the perpetrators of cyber blockades can come from any of the levels of analysis. Furthermore, because of the nature of cyberspace, the perpetrators of cyber attacks have a much greater ability to maintain anonymity or plausible deniability than belligerents in other types of blockades.

Cyber blockades have a nonphysical element that differentiates them from other types of blockades. Some of the infrastructure of cyberspace is physical and can be mechanically or manually manipulated, but much of the network is composed of digital topography that is man-made and subject to change. Thus, the partial nonphysicality of cyberspace presents a distinction for cyber blockades.

The time associated with blockades is also different in cyberspace. Cyber blockades can happen in seconds, and although more preparation time is required to develop the malware and organize the distribution of it, this does not require as much time as deploying or repositioning ships in preparation for a blockade. Aerial blockades are faster to establish than naval ones, but they are still likely to take more time to organize and coordinate than a cyber attack.

The second aspect of time is the duration of the cyber blockade. Cyber blockades can be relatively short—lasting for minutes, hours, or weeks— yet still sufficient to achieve its goals, whether they are to create damage to the political, economic, or social development of the country, or to demonstrate the perpetrators' capability and willingness to use cyber blockades as a tool of international relations. Duration is important for cyber blockades in that it must be long enough to achieve the attackers' goals, but there is not a specified threshold which a cyber attack must exceed in order to qualify as a blockade. This is consistent with international and customary law for other types of blockades, which also did not stipulate a period of duration of the blockade—it could last for days or years, depending on what was determined to be necessary and appropriate to achieve the blockader's goals. Although historical naval blockades tended to take longer to achieve their goals, there is no formal or legal requirement for a blockade to be imposed for a specified duration of time.

Cyber blockades also differ from traditional blockades in terms of cost. The true costs of cyber blockades are difficult to estimate because there are many different ways to construct a cyber blockade (mechanical, electromagnetic, and digital attacks), and each requires different resources and incurs different costs. Using the cyber attacks in Estonia and Georgia as a guide, rough estimates place botnets at 4 cents per machine. Whatever the mechanism for attack, it is likely that cyber blockades will still be less expensive to impose and maintain than blockades using ships or aircraft. Individual attackers participated often without knowing it (due to zombie computers), thus salaries did not need to be paid and lives were not put at risk. The political costs associated with cyber blockades could be quite high if the perpetrators were positively identified. This is an important caveat, though, because in the two case studies, the perpetrators were not identified, caught, or held accountable (with the exception of the one individual in Estonia), thus the political costs turned out to be quite low.

The resources needed to conduct cyber blockades differ from naval, aerial, or land blockades, but blockades in those domains also differ from each other. The important difference in resources is the ability of nonstate actors to access the resources necessary for cyber blockades. Traditionally, only large actors such as states or empires could raise the funds and acquire the resources necessary to conduct a blockade, but this is not the case with cyberspace.

Conclusion

The cases of Estonia and Georgia revealed many similarities in terms of the goals, actors, capabilities, preexisting conflict, and rights of neutrals, and both cases meet the criteria for blockades. In addition, cyber blockades fit within the essential criteria for blockades that were established with analysis of blockades in other domains. The analysis also reveals the critical differences of cyber blockades. These differences help deepen the understanding of the unique aspects of cyber blockades and the way in which technology affects blockade operations.

CHAPTER 7

Conclusion

Cyberspace is the modern information highway, and the bits and bytes of data that pass through it every day define power relationships throughout the world. Given how ubiquitous cyberspace is in modern life, governments, militaries, financial sectors, businesses, and social organizations heavily depend on cyberspace and its technologies for their essential daily operations. This growing dependence on cyberspace for all aspects of life in modern societies and in many developing societies means that exclusion from cyberspace would have a significant, adverse impact on their governments, businesses, militaries, and people.

Findings

Recognizing how important cyberspace is to daily life throughout the world, this book set out to foster an understanding of how states, corporations, and individuals can be cut off from cyberspace and its networks of power and communication. Using the historical examples of blockades in other domains as a guide, this research aimed to determine what would constitute a blockade in cyberspace.

Blockade law has changed significantly since it was first codified in the eighteenth century, and our understanding of blockade operations continues to be modified by current blockade practices on land, at sea, and in the air. In each domain, blockades employ different technologies and face challenges unique to that domain. As a result, blockades can be highly domain-specific, yet this research identified five factors that all blockades have in

< 141 >

common. (See Table 3.1 for the similarities of blockade operations in different domains.)

An additional comparison with blockades in other domains reveals that the cyber attacks on Estonia and Georgia fit within the scope of blockades, as defined in Chapter 3. The case studies reveal consistency and similarities in the actions, actors, capabilities, presence of conflict, and rights of neutrals across all domains examined, including cyberspace. These consistencies and similarities are displayed in Table 7.1. Thus, this research concludes that the cyber attacks on Estonia and Georgia in 2007 and 2008 are examples of cyber blockades.

To return briefly to the discussion of blockades and exclusion zones in Chapter 3, the analysis reveals that the cyber attacks fit into the scope of blockades and exclusion zones. In both Estonia and Georgia, external actors created conditions that denied access to and services of cyberspace within a geographic region. The denial of access was impartial (it did not discriminate among data packages based on their origin) and it was effective (some data did make it through, but this does not invalidate its effectiveness). Thus, we can conclude that the conditions for blockade in cyberspace were met in these cases.

The cyber attacks also interfered with the flow of data within the targeted states. As such, the cyber attacks also created "cyber exclusion zones" within Estonia and Georgia. This is important because exclusion zones have a disputed status under international law and they are not subject to the Law of Armed Conflict in the same way that blockades are. In particular, effectiveness is not a requirement for exclusion zones, which lowers the bar for determining if an exclusion zone has been created.

Conclusions

The following are several conclusions drawn from this research and analysis. The first two directly answer the questions posited in the first chapter, and the rest represent insights from the research that may further the development of a theory for cyber blockades or cyber warfare.

Conclusion 1: Cyber blockade is a situation rendered by an attack on cyber infrastructure or systems that prevents a state from accessing cyberspace, thus preventing the transmission (ingress/egress) of data beyond a geographical boundary. Cyber blockade is a legitimate tool of international statecraft and, consistent with other types of blockades, it can be considered

Table 7.1 Similarities among Blockade Operations in Six Different Domains

	Maritime	Aerial	Land	Space	Informational	Cyberspace
Actions	Prevent ingress/egress of ships or craft to or from ports or harbors	Prevent aircraft from entering an airspace or NFZ	Prevent entry to or exit from a specific city or region	Prevent entry into outer space	Prevent the transmission of information beyond national borders	Prevent the transmission of data beyond borders
Actors	States, independent territories	States, independent territories	States	States	States	States, nonstate actors, individuals
Capabilities	Superior maritime capabilities; knowledge of the domain and opponent's vulnerabilities	Superior aerial capabilities; knowledge of the domain and opponent's vulnerabilities	Superior land capabilities; knowledge of the domain and opponent's vulnerabilities	Superior technological or economic capabilities; knowledge of the opponent's vulnerabilities	Historically, sea-based capabilities to interfere with cables; knowledge of the domain and opponent's vulnerabilities	Technological capability; knowledge of the domain and opponent's vulnerabilities
Presence of Conflict	War or extant conflict	War or extant conflict	War	War or extant conflict	War	War or extant conflict
Role of Neutrals	Rights protected	Rights protected	Rights protected	Rights protected	Rights protected	Neutrals not specifically targeted, but consequences difficult to predict

an act of war (although it is ultimately up to the targeted state whether or not it *wants* to consider it an act of war and potentially escalate the situation).

Cyber blockade targets states in their entirety and tries to create massive outages. The goal of cyber blockades is to prevent the transmission of data beyond geographical borders through the manipulation, control, or dominance of cyberspace and its associated technologies in order to render political, economic, social, or psychological harm to the adversary. Cyberspace is a physical web that can be manipulated to punish adversaries by impeding their access to data traffic that is essential for security and prosperity, and cyber blockades are an effective means of denying or impeding access to cyberspace.

Conclusion 2: Actors use cyber blockades as tools of international relations because they are an effective, low-cost method of controlling an adversary's access to modern networks of power and can be conducted in such a way as to increase the perpetrator's anonymity or plausible deniability, thereby reducing the risk of retaliation. In addition, there are few alternative courses of action available to achieve the same result, especially for nonstate actors.

Conclusion 3: States, proxy groups, nonstate actors, or individuals can launch cyber blockades, if they have the capability and capacity. In the cases of Estonia and Georgia, the attackers were nonstate actors that most likely received support from Russia. However, groups that are not state-sponsored could also enact a cyber blockade if they possessed the proper technical skills to plan and coordinate a massive cyber attack directed at an entire state. Physical attacks on cyber infrastructure require few resources and little expertise; at a minimum, perpetrators must be able to locate and destroy key cyber infrastructure. Electromagnetic attacks are in the realm of state warfare and require significantly more resources to achieve. Thus, depending on how the cyber blockade is created (through digital, physical, or electromagnetic attacks), the threshold for capability to conduct a cyber attack can range from quite low (physically destroying cables or terminals) to high (electromagnetic attacks).

Conclusion 4: Cyber blockades can affect all aspects of cyberspace technologies, including electrical grids, power plants, regular telephone services, and mobile telephone services, among others. Cyber blockades, like other blockades, are intrinsically nonviolent, but they can result in damage, destruction, or death, depending on how they are implemented and their effects on targets. Targets classified as "restricted" under international law, such as hospitals, would continue to be restricted in cyberspace.

Conclusion 5: Cyber blockades can be created using mechanical, electromagnetic, or digital attacks. The cases examined in this research focused on cyber blockades conducted via digital attacks, but this is not the only way to implement a cyber blockade. Physical attacks are a viable alternative to digital attacks, and they constitute an act of violence under international law because they damage the physical infrastructure of cyberspace. Electromagnetic attacks are possible but perhaps less likely because they require greater resources; nonetheless, they remain an effective way to implement a cyber blockade.

Conclusion 6: As blunt instruments of warfare, cyber blockades are highly effective at achieving specific results, but they may not always be the tool of choice for actors. In certain situations, decision makers may favor more specialized types of cyber attacks that are highly sophisticated and precise and can achieve results such as espionage or destruction of a targeted system while preserving the integrity of other systems.

Conclusion 7: Cyber blockades can be established relatively quickly and for low cost, depending on the method of attack used. The speed and costs vary with the different types of cyber blockade (e.g., electromagnetic blockades require more resources than a physical blockade) but in general provide the offensive actor with the benefits of a high-speed and relatively low-cost option.

Conclusion 8: Cyber blockades are technically feasible against any country, but they are easier to achieve against geographically smaller countries. Larger countries typically have more connections to cyberspace, creating a more resilient network of connections between that country and other countries. As such, it would be more difficult to impose a cyber blockade against a larger, well-connected country than against a smaller country with fewer external cyber connections and a potentially less resilient system.

Conclusion 9: Cyber blockades may be considered a subset of informational blockades because they target the transmission of information. However, informational blockades are not widely recognized, so this categorization may not be the most useful for policymakers. In addition to being a subset of informational blockades, cyber blockades should also be considered separately because they occur within a specific domain and thus can benefit from cross-domain comparisons. Thus, cyber blockades are simultaneously domain-specific blockades for cyberspace and a subset of informational blockades.

Conclusion 10: Cyber blockades can be, but need not *always* be, considered acts of war. Context is key: Depending on the circumstances, cyber blockades may be considered pacific blockades. The evolution of blockades in other domains demonstrates that while most blockades have been considered acts of war between belligerents, pacific blockades are not acts of war. This corollary continues to be relevant for cyberspace; declaring war is inherently a political decision motivated by various factors.

Because cyber blockades interfere with state sovereignty, trade, communications, military operations, and other activities, they can rightly be considered an act of war, regardless of the physical destruction they generate. (It is worth remembering that blockades in other domains do not have to be violent or destructive to be considered blockades; they must only be effective in intercepting traffic.) However, pacific blockades are a form of coercive diplomacy where the blockading state declares that it does not seek to bring about war, but rather to compel the blockaded state to yield to demands made of it. It is highly conceivable that at some point in the near future the international community may seek to impose pacific cyber blockade as a form of sanction against states that violate international law.

Conclusion 11: Cyber blockades and cyber exclusion zones are two different types of operations. Cyber blockades are anti-access operations, whereas cyber exclusion zones are area-denial operations. Both have applicability to international politics and law, but they are not the same.[1]

Conclusion 12: The increased number and types of actors in cyberspace presents a complex situation for attribution and makes anonymity or plausible deniability possible at an unprecedented level in cyber warfare. While this is true for all aspects of cyberspace and cyber security efforts, it is particularly relevant for blockades because their potential impact is so severe. States cannot rely on the traditional model of deterrence against cyber blockades because they may not be able to identify the perpetrators, thus they must focus more on developing robust, redundant, and resilient systems that can withstand or recover quickly from a cyber blockade.

Conclusion 13: Public-private partnerships have special implications for cyber blockades because the domain of cyber space is not a pure public good—it is owned and operated primarily by private corporations or individuals, yet governments are charged with protecting it as part of the critical national infrastructure. Previous types of blockades involved the private sector to various degrees (e.g., merchant ships, commercial aircraft, or even telegraph cables), but cyber blockades represent the first time that the public and private interests have been intertwined to such an extent.

Conclusion 14: As the topology of cyberspace changes and actors modify their capabilities, the vulnerabilities associated with cyber blockades change as well. Improvements in technology will reduce vulnerabilities in some areas, whereas changes to cyberspace itself will likely reveal new vulnerabilities, which malicious actors will exploit.

Just as blockades evolved significantly over time, so we should expect the same to occur for cyber blockades. The maritime domain provides the compelling examples of evolution in blockade law and practice from the eighteenth century until today, but there have also been many developments and modifications of blockades in other domains. Cyber blockades will evolve as our understanding of the domain changes, technology makes new things possible, and the international community develops rules, norms, and laws that govern or regulate the use of cyberspace.

Recommendations

The recommendations based on the conclusions of research can be grouped into two categories: policy and scholarly recommendations. In many respects, there may be overlaps between the efforts of the policy community and academics that could be beneficial to the advancement of research on cyber blockades, but for the purposes of organization, these recommendations are introduced separately in this document.

For the Academic Community

As the academic community continues its research on cyberspace and cyber security, it is essential that it develops a shared terminology to discuss events and phenomena in cyberspace. Currently, the scholarly literatures is divided over definitions of the most basic terms, such as cyberspace, cyber attacks, cyber warfare, and the use of force. Consensus is beginning to emerge in certain areas, but it is essential that the scholarly community develop a consistent set of terminology to refer to facets of and events in cyberspace.

In that vein, scholars must be vigilant in refining and defining how historical experiences may or may not be appropriate for understanding cyberspace and security within it. This study drew extensively from the historical evolution of blockades and exclusion zones in other domains in order to define blockades in cyberspace and identify common features across domains. However, historical experiences and cross-domain comparisons were not always a perfect fit for cyber blockades, and in assessing any new developments, one must be aware that frequently there are additional factors or innovations that cannot be addressed through the historical paradigm.

For cyber blockades, the proliferation of actors at different levels of analysis, the role of anonymity, the speed of a cyber attack, and the cost of a cyber blockade all represent significant diversions from past experiences; their uniqueness and importance must be addressed but not overstated. Thus, it is important to be precise in balancing unique attributes of cyberspace with cross-domain theory applications or historical experiences in order to understand challenges in this particular domain. History has much to offer for framing new challenges, but the uniqueness of the domain and its attributes must be neither forgotten nor overstated in the pursuit of understanding.

As consensus is reached on the terminology of cyberspace, it is also important for the scholarly community to develop new theories or modify existing theories to explain and predict events in cyberspace. International relations theories are useful in shedding light on key elements of cyberspace, but a comprehensive approach to theory development would be useful to address all aspects of the domain. A comprehensive approach would "map" the aspects of the domain for future research and highlight linkages with extant scholarship.

For the Policy Community

Three recommendations for the policy community emerge from this research. The first recommendation is for policymakers and government officials to plan for scenarios in which access to cyberspace is denied for a significant period of time. Denial of access could be the result of an accident (as has been the case in the United States several times) or the result of an intentional attack on the nation's critical infrastructure. Although a situation that produces widespread denial of access may be unlikely in the United States, it would be a high-impact, hard-to-predict, rare event—the very definition of a "black swan" event.[2] Given the reliance of government and society on cyberspace for daily activities, many of which are so mundane and routine that they are often ignored or overlooked, it is difficult to justify *not* planning for a crisis in which access to cyberspace is attacked.

Second, international norms regarding acceptable behaviors and the use of force are critical for a common understanding of conflict. This research highlights that currently there is little international consensus regarding acceptable uses of cyberspace or cyber technologies. Many governments, intergovernmental organizations, and international organizations have begun discussions about this issue, but thus far it has proven difficult to achieve consensus on how cyberspace should and should not be used by states and nonstate actors.

This ambiguity presents difficulties during conflicts because actors do not have clear or common definitions of use of force in cyberspace. As a result, decision makers may hold different views of "red lines" for attack, leading to debates within states and among allies and risking unintended escalation of a conflict. Cyber blockades touch on just a small part of this larger debate by asking the question of whether blockades in cyberspace are considered an act of war.

This research argues that cyber blockade is a legitimate tool of statecraft. Cyber blockade conforms to historical experiences of blockade operations at sea, in the air, and on land, and it is consistent with the international law on blockade operations. Given the historical and legal precedents, there are many reasons to consider cyber blockade as part of the logical evolution of warfare in a new domain. As a legitimate tool of international relations, states alone would have the authority to implement cyber blockades. Rules for attribution would be helpful but are not strictly necessary (similar to rules pertaining to submarines). Furthermore, it would not be lawful for nonstate actors to engage in cyber blockades, just as they cannot lawfully engage in naval, aerial, or land blockades. Lastly, consistent with traditional understanding of blockade operations as acts of war, cyber blockades could also be considered acts of war.

Efforts to achieve domestic and international consensus on appropriate uses of cyberspace would benefit from a legal framework for cooperation to enforce the norms and standards agreed upon by signatories. Serious and urgent consideration must be given to determining what actions in cyberspace constitute a "use of force" or "armed attack" so that red lines can be established before conflicts begin and avert unintentional escalation. These efforts must also address active and passive defenses and retaliatory options for states that are the victims of cyber attacks.

The third and final area for potential policy advancement is the private-public partnership forum. In the United States, the private sector owns and operates more than 80 percent of the cyberspace infrastructure and technologies, yet the government plays a leading role in protecting this infrastructure and its systems. In the event of a cyber blockade against the United States, national security and commercial interests alike would be adversely affected.

Policymakers and government officials in the United States and other countries can develop a framework to address the security challenges that accompany cyberspace while still preserving the openness of the networks for commercial and private use. It is in no one's interest to have networks and cyber technologies that lack security or reliability, yet the overall effectiveness of the domain could be compromised by burdensome security requirements. Public and private sectors both stand to lose if cyberspace is not protected adequately, therefore the burden should be shared by actors from both sectors. The government can protect its own systems and networks as well as authorize, regulate, and enforce measures that provide incentives for the private sector to invest in security of commercial or private systems.

Closing

Blockades are not events of the past, relegated to sea stories and folklore. They have occurred within the most modern of environments and are likely to occur for as long as they continue to be effective. Modern information societies would benefit from planning to defend against cyber blockades and recover from them, if necessary. Policymakers must develop strategies that direct the use of cyber blockades and the appropriate responses to them. Scholars can look to the other features of cyberspace and ask what else has its roots in the past. Extant research on cyberspace and cyber security has laid a solid foundation for understanding the domain, its features, and the key actors within it.

Much more work lies ahead for integrating research on cyberspace with other theories about power, communication, and the role of information in the twenty-first century. The proliferation of nonstate actors raises new questions about the role of individuals and the rights of states in conflicts. As nonstate actors increasingly play a role in international politics, will the laws of armed conflict need to be modified to account for the role of civilians who initiate conflicts and take up arms on the physical or virtual battlefields? If anonymity can truly be maintained in cyberspace, what are the implications for power and conflict? Finally, the trend toward a "cybered Westphalian age" in which states delineate borders of their territory within the domain of cyberspace puts us on a path of norms and national interests being negotiated within and among states.[3] For the law-abiding citizens, the view of cyberspace as a national asset carries with it significant questions about the ability to preserve openness and accessibility while providing necessary security and protection against domestic and foreign threats.

The rapid expansion of cyberspace over the past decade has changed the way people, governments, and economies interact, and the implications of these changes offer fruitful ground for future research and innovation.

Notes

1. For a discussion of the differences between anti-access and area-denial operations, see Freier, "The Emerging Anti-Access/Area-Denial Challenge."
2. Taleb, *The Black Swan: The Impact of the Highly Improbable.*
3. Demchak and Dombrowski, "Rise of a Cybered Westphalian Age."

Glossary

Blockade: the isolation of a nation, area, city, or harbor by hostile forces in order to prevent the entrance and exit of traffic and commerce.

Botnets: a network of internet-connected programs or computers that are used to perform certain tasks. Many computers involved in botnets are zombies (computers infected with malware to gain control over the system and operate it without the owner's consent). Networks of zombie computers can be used to perform automated tasks, such as spread viruses and launch denial-of-service attacks.

Cyber attack: the "deliberate actions to alter, disrupt, deceive, degrade, or destroy computer systems or networks or the information and/or programs resident in or transiting these systems or networks."[1] In order to qualify as an *armed* attack under international law, an attack in cyberspace must result in damage, destruction, or death.[2]

Cyber blockade: a situation rendered by an attack on cyber infrastructure or systems that prevents a state from accessing cyberspace, thus preventing the transmission (ingress and egress) of data beyond a geographical boundary.

Cyber exploitation: surreptitiously obtaining confidential information via cyberspace. This includes a wide range of actions from official government spying to corporate espionage to individual-level identity theft.

Cyber power: the "ability to use cyberspace to create advantages and influence events in all the operational environments and across the instruments of power."[3]

Cyber warfare: a state of hostilities between countries or their agents (including organized nonstate groups under the control of the state) that involves cyber operations that result in damage, destruction, or death. Consistent with the law of armed conflict, cyber war can also come into existence without the presence

< 153 >

of hostilities: it is generally accepted that a declaration of war or the establishment of a blockade can initiate war.

Cyberspace: "a global domain within the information environment whose distinctive and unique character is framed by the use of electronics and the electromagnetic spectrum to create, store, modify, exchange, and exploit information via interdependent and interconnected networks using information-communication technology."[4] It is a partially man-made environment that consists of physical attributes (such as computers and cables) as well as digital attributes (such as bits and bytes of data) and uses information technology to manage information passed along networks that create a web of connections and interdependence. Cyberspace includes but is not limited to the internet (also known as the World Wide Web). Cyberspace also includes closed networks, such as the US government's Secure Internet Protocol Router Network and satellite systems, among other hardware and software networks.

DDoS attack: distributed denial-of-service attack: a coordinated effort that instructs multiple computers to launch simultaneous DoS attacks directed at the same target.

DoS attack: an attack that sends a flood of traffic to overwhelm a computer system or consume bandwidth, thereby interrupting the normal flow of traffic to and from the site.

TCP SYN flood: a type of denial-of-service attack in which the attacker sends a series of "SYN" requests to a target's computer in an attempt to consume the bandwidth with a bogus connection and render it inaccessible to legitimate traffic (TCP, transmission control protocol; SYN, synchronize message). This type of attack interrupts the protocol that requires a "three-way handshake" for packets to travel from point of origin to point of destination. As a result, the request for connection is never completed and the queue fills up, denying access to other users.

Notes

1. Owens, Dam, and Lin, *Technology, Policy, Law, and Ethics regarding U.S. Acquisition and Use of Cyberattack Capabilities*, 1.

2. Schmitt, ed. *The Tallinn Manual on the International Law Applicable to Cyber Warfare*.

3. Kuehl, "From Cyberspace to Cyberpower: Defining the Problem," 38.

4. Ibid., 28.

Bibliography

Adair, Steven. "Georgian Websites under Attack—DoS and Defacement." Shadowserver Foundation. http://www.shadowserver.org/wiki/pmwiki.php/Calendar/20080811.

———. "The Website for the President of Georgia under Attack—Politically Motivated?" Shadowserver Foundation. http://www.shadowserver.org/wiki/pmwiki.php/Calendar/20080720.

The American Heritage Dictionary of the English Language. 5th ed. Boston: Houghton Mifflin Harcourt, 2011.

Andress, Jason, Steve Winterfeld, and Russ Rogers. *Cyber Warfare: Techniques, Tactics and Tools for Security Practitioners.* Boston: Syngress/Elsevier, 2011.

Arquilla, John, David F. Ronfeldt, and US Department of Defense. Office of the Secretary of Defense. *Networks and Netwars: The Future of Terror, Crime, and Militancy.* Santa Monica, CA: Rand, 2001.

Ashmore, William C. "Impact of Alleged Russian Cyber Attacks." *Baltic Security and Defence Review* 11 (2009): 4–40.

Associated Press. "Third Internet Cable Cut in the Middle East." February 1, 2008.

Baer, George W. *One Hundred Years of Sea Power: The U.S. Navy, 1890–1990.* Stanford, CA: Stanford University Press, 1994.

Baker, Stewart, and Shaun Waterman. "In the Crossfire: Critical Infrastructure in the Age of Cyber War." McAfee. http://resources.mcafee.com/content/NACIPReport.

Baltic News Service. "Last Cyber Attacks against Estonia Take Place during Last Night." May 2, 2007.

———. "NATO Makes Statement Backing Estonia in Row with Russia." May 3, 2007.

———. "Te—02!.03.05.07 01.10 J.J. US Urges Russia to Back Off in War Memorial Dispute with Estonia." May 3, 2007.

———. "US Congressman Rises to Defend Estonia's Sovereignty." May 4, 2007.

———. "US, European Specialists Help Estonia Deal with Cyber Attacks." May 10, 2007.

< 155 >

————. "US Secretary of State Expresses Support to Estonia." May 3, 2007.

————. "US Senate Passes Resolution of Solidarity with Estonia." May 4, 2007.

Barnett, Roger W. "Technology and Naval Blockade: Past Impact and Future Prospects." *Naval War College Review* Summer 2005, 58, no. 3 (2005): 87–98.

Baryshnikov, N. I. (2003), Блокада Ленинграда и Финляндия 194–44 [Finland and the siege of Leningrad], Институт Йохана Бекмана.

BBC News. "The Cyber Raiders Hitting Estonia." May 15, 2007.

————. "Estonia Fines Man for 'Cyber War.'" January 25, 2008.

————. "Estonian Newspaper Says Russian Cyber Attacks Repelled." May 4, 2007.

————. "NATO Denies Georgia and Ukraine." April 3, 2008.

————. "Russia Army Unit Sent to Abkhazia." May 31, 2008.

Beale, Michael O. "Bombs over Bosnia: The Role of Airpower in Bosnia-Herzegovina." MMAS. School of Advanced Airpower Studies, 1997.

Bennhold, Katrin. "Differences Emerge in Europe of a Response to Georgia Conflict." *New York Times*, August 12, 2008.

Brenner, Susan W. *Cyberthreats: The Emerging Fault Lines of the Nation State.* New York: Oxford University Press, 2009.

Brodie, Bernard. *Sea Power in the Machine Age.* 2nd ed. Princeton, NJ: Princeton University Press, 1943.

Brüggemann, Karsten, and Andres Kasekamp. "The Politics of History and the 'War of Monuments' in Estonia." *Nationalities Papers: The Journal of Nationalism and Ethnicity* 36, no. 3 (July 2008): 425–48.

Carr, Edward Hallett, and Michael Cox. *The Twenty Years' Crisis, 1919–1939: An Introduction to the Study of International Relations.* New York: Palgrave MacMillan, 2001.

Carr, Jeffrey. *Inside Cyber Warfare.* 2nd ed. Sebastopol, CA: O'Reilly, 2012.

Carr, Jeff, et al. "Project Grey Goose: Phase I Report: Russia/Georgia Cyber War—Findings and Analysis." In *Project Grey Goose*, 24, 2008.

————. "Project Grey Goose Phase II Report: The Evolving State of Cyber Warfare." In *Project Grey Goose*: Greylogic, 2009.

Castells, Manuel. *Communication Power.* New York: Oxford University Press, 2009.

Clausewitz, Carl von. *On War.* Translated by Michael Howard and Peter Paret. Introduction by Beatrice Heuser. Oxford World's Classics. New York: Oxford University Press, 2006.

Coalson, Robert. "Behind the Estonia Cyberattacks." *Radio Free Europe Radio Liberty*, March 6, 2009.

Congress, 110th US. "Senate Resolution 187 (110th)." Government Printing Office, 2007.

Crowe, Eyre. "Memorandum on the Present State of British Relations with France and Germany." London, 1907.

Czosseck, Christian, and Kenneth Geers. *The Virtual Battlefield: Perspectives on Cyber Warfare*. Cryptology and Information Security Series. Washington, DC: IOS Press, 2009.

Daalder, Ivo H., and James G. Stavridis. "NATO's Success in Libya." *New York Times*, October 30, 2011.

Davis, Joshua. "Web War One: Hackers Take Down the Most Wired Country in Europe." *Wired* 15, no. 9 (2007). http://www.wired.com/print/politics/security/magazine/15-09/ff_estonia.

Demchak, Chris C., and Peter Dombrowski. "Rise of a Cybered Westphalian Age." *Strategic Studies Quarterly*, Spring 2011.

de Muth, Susan. "Israel's Own Goal: Susan De Muth Looks at the Truth behind the Israeli Media Hype Concerning the Gaza Flotilla Blockade, the Action That Saw a Turning of the Tide of World Opinion." *Middle East* August/September (2010). http://www.questia.com/PM.qst?a=o&d=5044455944.

De Seversky, Alexander Procofieff, and Rouben Mamoulian Collection (Library of Congress). *Victory through Air Power*. New York: Simon and Schuster, 1942.

Dougherty, James E., and Robert L. Pfaltzgraff. *Contending Theories of International Relations: A Comprehensive Survey*. 5th ed. New York: Longman, 2001.

Douhet, Giulio. *The Command of the Air*. Translated by Dino Ferrari. New York: Coward-McCann, 1942.

Dumbacker, Erin Dian. "Lessons from Estonia: Preparing for a Major Cyberattack." NextGov.com 2011.

Economist. "Mapping the Tubes." June 23, 2012.

———. "No Fly Zone in Libya: Will It Work?" March 18, 2011.

Ehin, Piret, and Eiki Berg. "Incompatible Identities? Baltic-Russian Relations and the EU as an Arena for Identity Conflict." In *Identity and Foreign Policy: Baltic-Russian Relations and European Integration*. Edited by Piret Ehin and Eiki Berg. Burlington, VT: Ashgate Publishing Company, 2009.

Ellemon, Bruce A. and S. C. M. Paine. *Naval Blockades and Seapower: Strategies and Counter-Strategies*. New York: Routledge, 2006.

Encyclopædia Britannica Online. "Siege of Leningrad."

Eshel, Tamir. "NATO Takes Control—Coordinating Air and Naval Blockade on Libya." Defense Update. http://defense-update.com/20110327_libya_report.html.

Espiner, Tom. "Georgia Accuses Russia of Coordinated Cyberattack." *CNET News*, August 11, 2008.

Europa. "European Commission's Crisis Response Assistance to Georgia in 2008 Reaches €120 Million." January 20, 2009.

European Parliament. "European Parliament Resolution on the Situation in Estonia." May 21, 2007.

European Union. "Summary on EU-Georgia Relations." http://eeas.europa.eu/georgia/eu_georgia_summary/index_en.htm.

Feifer, Gregory. "Estonia Seeks Stronger E.U. Response to Russia." *National Public Radio*, September 9, 2008.

Felgenhauer, Pavel. ""After August 7: The Escalation of the Russia-Georgia War." Chap. 9 in *The Guns of August 2008: Russia's War in Georgia*. Edited by Svante E. Cornell and S. Frederick Starr, 162–80. Armonk, NY: M.E. Sharpe, Inc., 2009.

Finn, Peter. "Cyber Assaults on Estonia Typify a New Battle Tactic." *Washington Post*, May 19, 2007.

———. "Russia's Moves Add to Strains with Georgia." *Washington Post*, May 1, 2008.

Fox News. "Estonia Charges Solo Hacker for Crippling Cyberattacks." January 25, 2008.

Freier, Nathan. "The Emerging Anti-Access/Area-Denial Challenge." Center for Strategic and International Studies, May 17, 2012.

Friedman, George. "The Russo-Georgian War and the Balance of Power." *Stratfor*, August 12, 2008.

Gerace, Michael P. *Military Power, Conflict, and Trade*. Portland, OR: Frank Cass Publishers, 2004.

Glaser, Charles L. "Deterrence of Cyber Attacks and US National Security," 8. Cyber Security Policy and Research Institute: The George Washington University, 2011.

Goble, Paul A. "Defining Victory and Defeat: The Information War between Russia and Georgia." Chap. 10 in *The Guns of August 2008: Russia's War in Georgia*. Edited by Svante E. Cornell and S. Frederick Starr, 181–95. Armonk, NY: M. E. Sharpe, Inc., 2009.

Golz, Thomas. "The Paradox of Living in Paradise: Georgia's Descent into Chaos." In *The Guns of August 2008: Russia's War in Georgia*. Edited by Svante E. Cornell and S. Frederick Starr, xiv, 279 pp., 10 pp. of plates. Armonk, NY: M. E. Sharpe, 2009.

Goodman, Will. "Cyber Deterrence: Tougher in Theory Than in Practice?" *Strategic Studies Quarterly* Fall (2010): 102–35.

Gouré, Leon. *The Siege of Leningrad*. Stanford, CA: Stanford University Press, 1962.

Guichard, Louis. *The Naval Blockade, 1914–1918*. Translated by Christopher Rede Turner. London: P. Allan & Co., Ltd., 1930.

Hafner-Burton, Emilie M., Miles Kahler, and Alexander H. Montgomery. "Network Analysis for International Relations." *International Organization* 63, no. 3 (2009): 559–92.

Hamilton, Mark D., Cdr., USN. "Blockade: Why This 19th Century Nelsonian Tool Remains Operationally Relevant Today." Naval War College, 2007.

Harding, Luke. "Protest by Kremlin as Police Quell Riots in Estonia." *Observer*, April 29, 2007.

Hays, Peter L. *United States Military Space: Into the Twenty-First Century*. Maxwell Air Force Base, AL: Air University Press, 2002.

Hollis, David. "Cyberwar Case Study: Georgia 2008." *Small Wars Journal*, January (2011).

Hyde, Charles Cheney. *International Law, Chiefly as Interpreted and Applied by the United States*. 2nd rev. ed. 3 vols. Boston, MA: Little, Brown and Company, 1945.

International Military Tribunal. *Nuremberg Trial Proceedings Vol. 8*. February 22, 1946.

International Telecommunications Union. "Percentage of Individuals Using the Internet 2000–2010." www.itu.int/ITU-/ict/statistics/material/excel/2010/IndividualsUsingInternet_00-10.xls.

Jackson, Patrick. "Playing Estonia's Political Cards." *BBC News*, May 12, 2007.

———. "Russian Roots and an Estonian Future." *BBC News*, May 10, 2007.

———. "When Giants Fought in Estonia." *BBC News*, May 9, 2007.

Johnson, Bobbie. "Faulty Cable Blacks out Internet for Millions." *Guardian*, January 30, 2008.

Johnson, Mike. "Georgian Websites under Attack—Don't Believe the Hype." Shadowserver Foundation. http://www.shadowserver.org/wiki/pmwiki.php/Calendar/20080812.

Kaldor, Mary. *New and Old Wars: Organized Violence in a Global Era*. Stanford, CA: Stanford University Press, 1999.

Karon, Tony. "The Georgia Crisis: A Blow to NATO." *Time*, August 15, 2008.

Kasekamp, Andres, and Martin Saeter. *Estonian Membership in the EU: Security and Foreign Policy Aspects*. Oslo: Norwegian Institute of International Affairs, 2003.

Kern, Paul Bentley. *Ancient Siege Warfare*. Bloomington, IN: Indiana University Press, 1999.

Knesset. "The Second Lebanese War." http://www.knesset.gov.il/lexicon/eng/Lebanon_war2_eng.htm.

Knorr, Klaus. *The Power of Nations: The Political Economy of International Relations*. New York: Basic Books, 1975.

Koppel, Ott. "Impact of Russian Hidden Economic Sanctions on Estonian Railway Transport," 26–30. Tallinn, Estonia: Tallinn University of Technology, 2008.

Korns, Stephen W., and Joshua E. Kastenberg. "Georgia's Cyber Left Hook." *Parameters,* Winter 2008–2009 (2009): 30–76.

Kramer, Franklin D., Stuart H. Hall, and Larry K. Wentz. *Cyberpower and National Security.* Washington, DC: National Defense UP, 2009.

Krebs, Brian. "Report: Russian Hacker Forums Fueled Georgia Cyber Attacks." *Washington Post*, October 16, 2008.

Krepon, Michael, Theresa Hitchens, and Michael Katz-Hyman. "Preserving Freedom of Action in Space: Realizing the Potential and Limits of U.S. Spacepower." Chap. 6 in *Toward a Theory of Spacepower*. Edited by Charles D. Lutes and Peter L. Hays, 119–54. Washington, DC: National Defense University Press, 2011.

Kuehl, Daniel T. "From Cyberspace to Cyberpower: Defining the Problem." Chap. 2 in *Cyberpower and National Security*. Edited by Franklin D. Kramer, Stuart H. Starr, and Larry K. Wentz, 24–42. Washington, DC: National Defense University Press and Potomac Books Inc., 2009.

Kurtbag, Ömer. "E.U.'s Response to the Georgian Crisis: An Active Peace Broker or a Confused and Divided Actor?" *Orta Asya ve Kafkasya Araştırmaları (OAKA)* [Journal of Central Asian & Caucasian Studies] 3, no. 6 (2008): 58–74.

Lambeth, Benjamin S. "Airpower, Spacepower, and Cyberpower." Chap. 8 in *Toward a Theory of Cyberpower*. Edited by Charles D. Lutes and Peter L. Hays, 155–78. Washington, DC: National Defense University Press, 2011.

Landler, Mark, and John Markoff. "Digital Fears Emerge after Data Siege in Estonia." *New York Times*, May 29, 2007.

Levy, Clifford J. "Russia Backs Independence of Georgian Enclaves." *New York Times*, August 26, 2008.

Lewis, James A. "Thresholds for Cyber War," 9. Washington, DC: Center for Strategic and International Studies, 2010.

Libicki, Martin C., and Project Air Force (US). *Cyberdeterrence and Cyberwar*. Santa Monica, CA: RAND, 2009.

MacFarquhar, Neil, and Ethan Bronner. "Report Finds Naval Blockade of Israel Legal but Faults Raid." *New York Times*, September 1 2011.

Mackinder, Halford J. "The Geographical Pivot of History." *Geographical Journal*, no. 23 (1904): 421–37.

MacMillan, Norman. "Air Blockade: What Are Its Possibilities and Difficulties?" *Air Strategy* XI (July 18 1940): 2.

Mahan, Alfred Thayer. "Blockade in Relation to Naval Strategy." *Proceedings* 12, no. 4 (1895): 851–66.

———. *The Influence of Sea Power Upon History, 1660–1783*. 6th ed. Boston: Little, Brown, and Company, 1894.

Markoff, John. "Before the Gunfire, Cyberattacks." *New York Times*, August 12, 2008.

Martel, William C. *Victory in War: Foundations of Modern Strategy*. New York: Cambridge University Press, 2011.

McLaughlin, Daniel. "Estonia Closes Moscow Embassy as President Berates Russia." *Irish Times*, May 3, 2007.

Mearsheimer, John J. *The Tragedy of Great Power Politics*. New York: Norton, 2001.

Medlicott, W. N. *The Economic Blockade*. History of the Second World War United Kingdom Civil Series. 2 vols. London: H. M. Stationery Office, 1952.

Miller, Roger G. *To Save a City: The Berlin Airlift, 1948–1949*. College Station, TX: Texas A&M University Press, 2000.

Morozov, Evgeny. *The Net Delusion: The Dark Side of Internet Freedom*. 1st ed. New York: Public Affairs, 2011.

Nakashima, Ellen. "U.S. Said to Be Target of Massive Cyber-Espionage Campaign." *Washington Post*, February 10, 2013.

Nazario, Jose. "Georgia DDoS Attacks—A Quick Summary of Observations." *DDoS and Security Reports: The Arbor Networks Security Blog* (April 12, 2008). http://ddos.arbornetworks.com/2008/08/georgia-ddos-attacks-a-quick -summary-of-observations/.

———. "Political DDoS: Estonia and Beyond." 2008. http://static.usenix.org/ event/sec08/tech/slides/nazario-slides.pdf.

———. "Politically Motivated Denial of Service Attacks." In *The Virtual Battlefield: Perspectives on Cyber Warfare*. Edited by Christian Czosseck and Kenneth Geers. Cryptology and Information Security Series. Washington, DC: IOS Press, 2009.

Nilsson, Niklas. "Georgia's Rose Revolution: The Break with the Past." In *The Guns of August 2008: Russia's War in Georgia*. Edited by Svante E. Cornell and S. Frederick Starr, xiv, 279 pp., 10 pp. of plates. Armonk, N.Y.: M. E. Sharpe, 2009.

North Atlantic Treaty Organization. "NATO and Libya—Operation Unified Protector." http://www.nato.int/cps/en/SID-F6CC01E5-5CEF1D22/natolive/ 71679.htm.

———. "NATO's Foreign Ministers Reiterate Their Support for Georgia." http://www.nato.int/docu/update/2008/08-august/e0819a.html.

———. "NATO's Relations with Georgia." http://www.nato.int/cps/en/natolive/ topics_38988.htm.

Nye, Joseph S., and Harvard University Center for International Affairs. *Peace in Parts: Integration and Conflict in Regional Organization*. Perspectives on International Relations. Boston, MA: Little, 1971.

O'Hanlon, Michael E. "Balancing US Security Interests in Space." Chap. 7 in *Toward a Theory of Spacepower*. Edited by Charles D. Lutes and Peter L. Hays, 137–54. Washington, DC: National Defense University Press, 2011.

Olson, Parmy. "'Biggest Cyber Attack in History' Could Have Been Carried out with Just a Laptop." *Forbes.com*, March 27, 2013.

Oltsik, Jon. "Russian Cyber Attack on Georgia: Lessons Learned?" Network World. http://www.networkworld.com/community/node/44448.

Oppenheim, L., and Hersch Lauterpacht. *International Law: A Treatise*. 8th ed. New York: Longmans, 1955.

Owens, William A., Kenneth W. Dam, and Herbert Lin. *Technology, Policy, Law, and Ethics regarding U.S. Acquisition and Use of Cyberattack Capabilities.* Washington, DC: National Academies Press, 2009.

Pace, Eric. "Confrontation in the Gulf; U.N. Call on Navies to Block Iraq's Trade; Resolution Permits Use of Force, U.S. Says." *New York Times*, August 26, 1990.

Palmer, Sir Geoffrey. "Report of the Secretary-General's Panel of Inquiry on the 31 May 2011 Flotilla Incident." United Nations. http://graphics8.nytimes.com/packages/pdf/world/Palmer-Committee-Final-report.pdf.

Parmelee, Maurice. *Blockade and Sea Power: The Blockade, 1914–1919, and Its Significance for a World State.* New York: Thomas Y. Crowell Company, 1924.

Pau, Louis-Francois. "Business and Social Evaluations of Denial of Service Attacks in View of Scaling Economic Countermeasures." In *The Virtual Battlefield: Perspectives on Cyber Warfare.* Edited by Christian Czosseck and Kenneth Geers. Washington, DC: IOS Press, 2009.

Pfaltzgraff, Robert L. "International Relations Theory and Spacepower." Chap. 3 in *Toward a Theory of Spacepower.* Edited by Charles D. Lutes and Peter L. Hays, 37–56. Washington, DC: National Defense University Press, 2011.

Poulsen, Kevin. "Estonia Drops Cyberwar Theory, Claims Packets Were 'Terrorism.'" *Wired.* http://www.wired.com/threatlevel/2007/06/estonia_drops_c/.

Program on Humanitarian Policy and Conflict Research at Harvard University. "Commentary on the HPCR Manual on International Law Applicable to Air and Missile Warfare." Bern, Switzerland, 2010.

Raab, Jorg. "Heading toward a Society of Networks: Empirical Developments and Theoretical Challenges." *Journal of Management Inquiry*, September no. 18 (2009): 198–210.

Raab, Jorg, and H. Brinton Milward. "Dark Networks as Problems." *Journal of Public Administration Research and Theory* 13, no. 4 (2003).

Rand, Erik, and Aivar Pau. "Paet: Russia Is Attacking EU through Estonia; According to Foreign Minister, Attack Is Virtual, Psychological, and Real, All at Once." *Eesti Paevaleht*, May 1, 2007.

Rattray, Gregory J. *Strategic Warfare in Cyberspace.* Cambridge, MA: MIT Press, 2001.

Rediff India Abroad. "Nashi, Russia's New Military Nationalist Movement." 2007. http://www.rediff.com/news/2007/may/21nashi.htm.

Regional Headquarters of Allied Forces Southern Command (NATO). "AFSOUTH Factsheet: Operation Deny Flight." http://www.afsouth.nato.int/archives/operations/DenyFlight/DenyFlightFactSheet.htm.

Rid, Thomas. *Cyber War Will Not Take Place.* New York, NY: Oxford University Press, 2013.

Rosa, Hartmut, and William E. Scheuerman. *High-Speed Society: Social Acceleration, Power, and Modernity.* University Park, PA: Pennsylvania State University Press, 2009.

Roth, Mathias. "Bilateral Disputes between E.U. Member States and Russia," 32. Brussels: Centre for European Policy Studies, 2009.

Rt.com. "Russia to Consider Sanctions against Estonia." http://rt.com/news/russia-to-consider-sanctions-against-estonia/.

"Russian Invasion of Georgia: Russian Cyberwar on Georgia." www.georgia update.gov.ge.

Salisbury, Harrison E. *The 900 Days; The Siege of Leningrad.* 1st ed. New York: Harper & Row, 1969.

Scheinman, Lawrence, and David A. Wilkinson. *International Law and Political Crisis: An Analytic Casebook.* Boston, MA: Little, 1968.

Schmitt, Michael, ed. *The Tallinn Manual on the International Law Applicable to Cyber Warfare.* New York: Cambridge University Press, 2013.

Schwartz, Mathew J. "Egypt Takes $90 Million Hit from Internet Blackout." *Information Week* (February 3, 2011). http://www.informationweek.com/news/security/management/229201128.

Shchedrov, Oleg, and Christian Lowe. "Russia Army Vows Steps if Georgia and Ukraine Join NATO." *Reuters*, April 11, 2008.

Sherr, James. "The Implications of the Russia-Georgia War for European Security." Chap. 11 in *The Guns of August 2008: Russia's War in Georgia.* Edited by Svante E. Cornell and S. Frederick Starr, 196–224. Armonk, NY: M.E. Sharpe, Inc., 2009.

Siney, Marion C. *The Allied Blockade of Germany, 1914–1916.* Ann Arbor, MI: University of Michigan Press, 1957.

Slider, Darrell. "Democratization in Georgia." In *Conflict, Cleavage, and Change in Central Asia and the Caucasus: Democratization and Authoritarianism in Postcommunist Societies.* Edited by Karen Dawisha and Bruce Parrott, xviii, 423 pp. New York: Cambridge University Press, 1997.

Slim, Hugo. *Killing Civilians: Method, Madness, and Morality in War.* New York: Columbia University Press, 2008.

Sontag, Sherry, Christopher Drew, and Annette Lawrence Drew. *Blind Man's Bluff: The Untold Story of American Submarine Espionage.* Thorndike Large-Print Americana Series. Thorndike, ME: Thorndike Press, 1999.

Stiennon, Richard. *Surviving Cyberwar.* Lanham, MD: Government Institutes, 2010.

Symonds, Craig L. *The Civil War at Sea.* Reflections on the Civil War Era. Santa Barbara, CA: Praeger, 2009.

Taleb, Nassim. *The Black Swan: The Impact of the Highly Improbable.* 2nd ed. New York: Random House Trade Paperbacks, 2010.

Telegraph. "NATO Ends 'Most Successful' Libya Mission." October 31, 2011.

Tikk, Eneken, et al. "Cyber Attacks against Georgia: Legal Lessons Identified," 46. Tallinn: Cooperative Cyber Defence Centre of Excellence, NATO, 2008.

Traynor, Ian. "Russia Accused of Unleashing Cyberwar to Disable Estonia: Parliament, Ministries, Banks, Media Targeted: NATO Experts Sent in to Strengthen Defences." *Guardian*, May 17, 2007.

Ukrainian News Agency. "Georgia Interested in Using Poti-Varna Fiber-Optic Cable for Joint Telecommunications Projects with Ukraine." May 18, 2012.

United Nations Office for the Coordination of Humanitarian Affairs. "Easing the Blockade—Assessing the Humanitarian Impact on the Population of the Gaza Strip." 2011.

United Nations Relief and Works Agency for Palestinian Refugees. "2012 U.N.W.R.A. Emergency Appeal." http://www.unrwa.org/userfiles/2011120681236.pdf.

United Nations Security Council. "Security Council Resolution 665 (1990)." 1990.

———. "Security Council Resolution 688 (1991)." 1991.

———. "Security Council Resolution 816 (1993)." 1993.

———. "Security Council Resolution 1973 (2011)." 2011.

US Central Command. "Full Organization Authority Record." National Archives.

US Central Intelligence Agency. "The World Factbook: Estonia." https://www.cia.gov/library/publications/the-world-factbook/geos/en.html.

US Department of Defense. "Joint Publication 1-02." August 2011.

US Department of State. "Background Note: Estonia." http://www.state.gov/r/pa/ei/bgn/5377.htm#political.

US Navy, Marine Corps, and Coast Guard. "The Commander's Handbook on the Law of Naval Operations (Nwp 1-14m, Mcwp 5-12.1, Comdtpub P5800.7a)." Edited by Department of the Navy and Department of Homeland Security, 184. Washington, DC: Government Printing Office, 2007.

USA Today. "Lebanon Air Blockade Lifted; Naval Blockade Stays in Place for Now." September 7, 2006.

Van Creveld, Martin. *The Transformation of War.* New York: The Free Press, Simon and Schuster Inc., 1991.

Van Evera, Stephen. *Guide to Methods for Students of Political Science.* Ithaca: Cornell University Press, 1997.

White, Mark J. *The Cuban Missile Crisis.* Basingstoke, UK: Macmillan, 1996.

White House. "International Strategy for Cyberspace." May 2011.

Wikipedia. "File:Georgia High Detail Map.Png." http://en.wikipedia.org/wiki/File:Georgia_high_detail_map.png.

———. "Siege of Leningrad." http://en.wikipedia.org/wiki/Siege_of_Leningrad.

Winkler, Jonathan Reed. *Nexus: Strategic Communications and American Security in World War I.* Harvard Historical Studies. Cambridge, MA: Harvard University Press, 2008.

Woehrel, Steven. "Estonia: Current Issues and U.S. Policy." In *CRS Report for Congress.* Washington, DC: Library of Congress, Congressional Research Services, 2007.

Womack, Helen. "NATO Joins U.S. in Condemning Russia's Response in South Ossetia." *Guardian*, August 11, 2008.

Wrenn, Christopher. "Strategic Cyber Deterrence." Tufts University, 2012.

Wu, Yuan-li. *Economic Warfare*. Prentice Hall Economics Series. New York: Prentice Hall, 1952.

Zarakhovich, Yuri. "Will Russia Block Kosovo Independence?" *Time*, May 23, 2007.

Ziemke, Earl. "Siege of Leningrad." In *The Oxford Companion to World War II*. Edited by I. C. B. Dear and M. R. D. Foot. Oxford Reference Online: Oxford University Press, 2001.

Zmijewski, Earl. "Georgia Clings to the 'Net." Renesys Blog. http://www .renesys.com/blog/2008/08/georgia_clings_to_the_net.shtml.

"Hacked by: Матричные Войны" [Hacked by: Matrix Wars]. Интерфакс [Interfax]. http://www.interfax.ru/society/txt.asp?id=26638.

 "Депутат Госдумы Признался, Что Эстонские Сайты Завалил Его Помощник" [State Duma deputy admitted that Estonian websites were blocked by his assistant]. SecurityLab by Positive Technologies. http://www.securitylab.ru/news/369590.php.

"Информационная Блокада" [Information blockade]. Век [Century]. http://wek.ru/cultura/69867-informacionnaya-blokada.html.

"Кальюранд: Кремлевская Администрация Атакует Эстонские Сайты" [Kaljurand: The Kremlin administration is attacking Estonian websites]. Грани.ру [Grani.ru]. http://www.grani.ru/Events/m.121465.html.

"На Сайте Мид Грузии Появился Коллаж С Гитлером" [A photo collage with Hitler appeared on the webpage of the Georgian Foreign Ministry]. Лента.ру [Lanta.ru]. http://www.lenta.ru/news/2008/08/09/defaced/.

"Сайты Риа Новости Подвергаются Непрерывным Dos-Атакам" [Websites of Ria Novosti are under continuous DoS attacks]. РИА Новости [RIA News]. http://ria.ru/news_company/20080810/150243787.html.

"У Здания Грузинского Посольства В Москве Разбит Палаточный Городок" [A tent camp in front of the building of the Georgian embassy]. Лента.Ру [Lenta.ru]. http://lenta.ru/news/2008/08/08/tents/.

"Заявление Совета Федерации Федерального Собрания Российской Федерации В Связи С Ситуацией Вокруг Памятника Воину-Освободителю В Таллине" [Statement of the Council of the Federal Assembly of the Russian Federation in connection with the situation around the Soldier Liberator Monument in Tallinn]. Управление по связям с общественностью и взаимодействию со СМИ [Office of Public Relations and Media Relations]. http://www.latvia.mid.ru/news/ru/07_007.html.

Index

< 167 >